The Black Pool

'Raw and powerful'
Irish Times, Books to look out for in 2025

'A funny, nerve-wracking and utterly compelling memoir of addiction and literature written in a language that is entanglingly inventive, at once cool and lush, and equally capable of conjuring the most delicate sense-memory and hardest heartbreak'
Colin Barrett, author of *Wild Houses*

'I've never read anything like *The Black Pool*. There are spiritual echoes of William S. Burroughs and Hunter S. Thompson, and of Sylvia Plath's jocose auto-fictional revelations of her efforts to die and to live, but these sentences are all Tim MacGabhann's own, and each one is a joyful thrill. His language is flamboyant, huge, dexterous, as alive as ink on paper can be. This is a wildly brilliant account of a life lived in a struggle against terrible pain, a memoir of addiction and recovery for the ages, a stone-cold classic of the form. I was floored by the power and beauty of this book'
Donal Ryan, author of *The Queen of Dirt Island*

'*The Black Pool* is extraordinary; MacGabhann manages to be simultaneously tender, raw, profound, hilarious and horrible, guiding us through a nightmare into beautiful, hard-won wisdom'
Lisa McInerney, author of *The Glorious Heresies*

'Tim MacGabhann uses language with such striking precision and verve, I would, in all honesty, happily read him on even the most banal and benign of subjects. *The Black Pool* is anything but that. And don't I just love the pitiless clarity of it, the unexpected turns of tenderness, the vitality at its core? This memoir of pain, addiction – and so much more – is a reading experience of the highest order'

Wendy Erskine, author of *Dance Move*

'The profundity of *The Black Pool* is this: it is made out of a clarity so violent that it reminds the reader, who exists but has likely grown used to existing, how utterly strange and difficult it is to exist, and how thin is the membrane between dailiness and an abyss. An extraordinary memoir by a writer with a rare gift. I feel changed by it'

Belinda McKeon, author of *Solace*

'*The Black Pool* is a bitter, truthful, painful account of life marred by addiction, and all the self-hatred it both masks and exacerbates'

Rob Doyle, author of *Here Are the Young Men*

'Every sentence is a still-burning roach, flicked with glee into the face of death. Only Tim MacGabhann can break your heart like this – and give you the language to stitch it back together. I urge you to succumb to the ice-cold, visceral glory of *The Black Pool*'

Ben Pester, author of *Am I in the Right Place?*

'I found this book beautiful, wild, poetical, with lashings of hilarity soaking every page and surprises leaping from every line. It's a desperately important book by a writer in the prime of their abilities. This writer shows us gruesome darkness just as he wills us to survive it all. Bravo, a shot in the arm'
Maggie Armstrong, author of *Old Romantics*

'Unflinchingly honest, heart-wrenching and life-affirming'
RTÉ, 10 books we're looking forward to reading

'MacGabhann traces the roots of addiction and illness through his youth and childhood, writing about where he tried to find solace and what happened when everything fell apart. A vibrant, darkly humorous writer'
Irish Independent, Non-fiction highlights for 2025

'A gripping and personal story of addiction'
Irish Examiner, 2025 Books to Read

Tim MacGabhann is the author of the novels *Call Him Mine* and *How to Be Nowhere*, the long poem *Rory Gallagher—Live!—from the Hotel of the Dead* and the memoir *The Black Pool*.

The Black Pool

A Memoir of Forgetting

Tim MacGabhann

Sceptre

First published in Great Britain in 2025 by Sceptre
An imprint of Hodder & Stoughton Limited
An Hachette UK company

The authorised representative in the EEA is Hachette Ireland, 8 Castlecourt Centre,
Dublin 15, D15 XTP3, Ireland (email: info@hbgi.ie)

1

A CIP catalogue record for this title is available from the British Library

Hardback ISBN 9781399728232
Trade Paperback ISBN 9781399728249
ebook ISBN 9781399728263

Typeset in Sabon by Manipal Technologies Limited

Printed and bound in Great Britain by Clays Ltd, Elcograf S.p.A.

Hodder & Stoughton policy is to use papers that are natural, renewable and
recyclable products and made from wood grown in sustainable forests. The logging
and manufacturing processes are expected to conform to the environmental
regulations of the country of origin.

Hodder & Stoughton Limited
Carmelite House
50 Victoria Embankment
London EC4Y 0DZ

www.sceptrebooks.co.uk

To Those Who Did Not Go Back –
Whose Bones being Nowhere,

Who is it that drags this corpse around?

Hsu Yun

'See the thing with me is that I actually really like Buddhism,' I said. I'd passed out on the plane from Brasília to Buenos Aires and come round to a large monk in orange robes squinting past my shoulder at the view of the runway. I'd asked him if we'd landed. He'd said we hadn't even taken off and I had groaned and felt a greasy weight of dread shunt down into my stomach. Then I'd said the thing about really liking Buddhism.

'Buddhism,' the monk said gravely. 'Is that so.' He rechecked his seatbelt. We'd been sitting there for the guts of two hours and the way every dunt of the storm shook the plane told me we'd be there for the guts of a couple more. I'd been waiting to leave Brasília for six weeks. My girlfriend had left me for someone else. My bank card had been cloned. The new one had taken two weeks and the new PIN a further month to arrive. I'd been offered a job in Mexico thanks to help from a friend but my work permit had yet to come through: in the meantime, my visa for Brazil had run out. So the idea was to go to Buenos Aires and wait for news from the school. Now the plane I was on to take me out of there wasn't leaving. I wondered if I was dead and in hell.

'Oh, yeah,' I said. I craned into the aisle, waggling my empty wine glass at nobody in particular. A drop

I

splashed on the webbing between finger and thumb and I kissed it off. It was as though I'd died six weeks before. That meant I had passed through the greenish stage of saponification, the leathery tightness where flesh had lost fat, all the way to the phase of burnt-black-looking femurs and ulnas and ribcage. I'd already shunted from Dublin to Barcelona to Brazil with my two big bags and two small bags; I'd shunt on yet to Buenos Aires; from there it'd be on to Uruguay and then at last Mexico City, hauling up my possessions all in one go every time. I was a white knuckle of pure tense desperation speeding through nowhere at such a speed that I sometimes mistook the sensation for hope. This was what rattling on the seat beside the monk felt like.

'Tell me more,' said the monk. He steepled his hands on his belly, just over the buckle of his belt, 'about what you know of Buddhism.'

'I saw this Buddha picture once,' I said. 'Buddha coming back as a hungry ghost to help the other hungry ghosts out of the pit. Horrible picture: a blue giant sitting lotus, mouth open, fangs showing, eyes hungry, but with a flat hunger, the way a dog looks, and the fangs showing, also the way a dog looks, how they are not quite smiling, just receiving something that fills a hunger, just this blue, huge giant, veins on the outside, mountainous guts, skin rippling, big fat entrail coils. And he's sitting in a meadow, surrounded by ring after ring of other, smaller demons, some decked in garlands of flowers, others wearing rings and necklaces and others throwing petals over one another, approaching a circle of smaller demons – their bellies bloated, their ribs showing, their whole torsos like barrels straining towards breakage – who are twisted and bent, the knuckles of their spines ridging through their skins, and yet with peaceful eyes, peaceful faces, meditating with the giant Buddha. And I remember seeing this and thinking, *Oh, no, is this it? Is this really all there is to it?*' I tugged at the collar of my shirt and wafted it but this did nothing, only sent the rotten-vegetable tang of my own pores up towards me. 'Is that you people? Is that one of yours?'

'Oh yes,' said the monk brightly. 'That's us alright.' He poured himself a measure of Guaraná from a soda can and seemed to be looking with affection at it. This jarred with me. If all attachment was suffering and all sensation brought attachment, then what was he doing adding to it by enjoying a delicious, chilled glass of Guaraná? He had a problem. I needed to dash this glass from his hand. He caught me looking at it.

'Want some?' he said.

'I think it would mix weird with my wine.'

'I suppose it would. But you don't have any.'

'I'm trying to fix that.' I leaned into the aisle again. The refreshments cart was making a slow second round of the plane, which was now a fug of shouty children, carping old people and awful men in business suits loosening their ties and leaning against the overhead bins to make important calls or, at least, to make calls sound important. The aircon groaned. Gusts of water vapour broke over us all but they were warmish now. The storm was a roar that pulled the air inside the plane taut against my head. I thought my skull might burst. The feeling of being already dead was back. It wasn't one of those giving up the ghost lightness of relief feelings. It was a sandbag-heavy exhaustion, as though I'd to carry my own corpse to its grave, because nobody else would. How I'd been able to haul myself over the concourse and onto the plane should have been a mystery in such circumstances but it was not. I'd simply gotten so drunk all morning that my body no longer felt like a body. But now the drink was wearing off and I was feeling dead again – cuffed to a corpse that happened to have my face. This happened so often it was ridiculous. It happened when I was coming back from the shop. It happened when I was on the subway. It happened when I was in the shower. It would leave me standing catatonic amid shelves, in sun glare, on the bathroom mat, under a towel I'd pulled from the hook on the wall, unable to do anything but wait until I was dry, too tired or hungover or drained or whatever even to think about eating: too tired, even, to contemplate the full list of small gestures required to get all the way from bed to food, as though each task – lift head, lift towel, towel head – only divided the distance between itself and the next by half, defeating all possibility of motion. I asked myself how I hadn't starved but maybe that was just thanks to the stubborn wish not to let my ex have the bragging rights over dragging some doggish gobshite over from Ireland and then starving him to death by breaking up with him. Spite was all that had me fastened to life.

I goggled at the monk. I wasn't sure how much I'd said of what I'd been thinking: perhaps quite a lot, to go by the look on his face.

The monk shrugged and spread his hands and said, 'Well, in some ways, yes, but it's not. Well. You can just sort of . . . breathe through it, really.'

The monk had a Dutch accent. He told me he'd moved to Indonesia as a hippie in the late sixties and become a monk. He gave talks and workshops all around the world. He said he enjoyed it, even though 'all beautiful places look the same'.

My forehead ran with sweat and my armpits felt all jungly. Rain strafed the concrete. On the horizon was that reddish smoke you get in Brasília, all that savannah mud beaten into the air.

*

I couldn't remember the taxi to the airport. The last thing I could remember before waking up on the plane was reaching for a spoon and the revolver-shaped novelty blowtorch lighter I had bought in Barcelona and letting it crackle under the foil again. I bent towards the fat clump of gritty powder. Snort, smoke, bang up, it all hit the same, at least at first, that stinging inverse rain, hot as comets, and molten, with a deep bassy whoosh powering each particle of my nasal tissues and the back of my neck, and then I'd be a galaxy inside lost to a rumble so pillowy in its texture that it may as well have been silence. White needles rushed my vision. The taste was a wire-thin pain jolting and jostling the nested coals of my brain until they shook down into the heat opening my lungs. The light shook. The world shook. I leaned back in the chair and kept going, melting through the plastic

5

threads of the back of it, all the way through the floor, the empty spaces of the apartments below, faster and faster, whoosh, whoosh, whoosh, a lift with the cable cut, a fall so hard the air gasped, through the basement of the underground car park where surely any day now my bank card and my PIN would come in the post, and then down through the gritty concrete seam separating the car park, into the telluric odours below: down, down beyond the clogged underearth and its pipes and cables into the moving red slicks of the mud beneath, there to land, settle, drift, dissolve, become consubstantial with the hidden bloodlayer flowing beneath it all – out of view, gone at last.

*

'And where did you see this picture?' said the monk.

'An encyclopaedia,' I said, 'at my grandfather's house. There were these big wooden masks with big teeth and overbites. Gnashy sort of a look to them. Popping eyes. Same as the giant I guess.'

The monk nodded and looked at me steadily through his steel-rim glasses. The lenses were tinted a gentle orange. A Dutch monk in orange glasses, I thought. Come on, man. It was just the kind of overliteral shit my dying brain might produce all by itself.

'Well, you know, we don't go in for these so much in Indonesia,' said the monk. 'It's a little quieter. A little less heavy metal.' He cycled his hands in the air over his lap. 'But it is all – the same. You know. Nirvana, samsara. The same thing.' He flicked his fingers outwards. 'No big deal.'

I thought to myself that this was among the more Dutch things I'd ever heard – the universe's entire metaphysical tangle reduced to 'not a big deal': a choice between desserts, almost. What must it be like to have come up in a world so solid and smooth that this was how it all felt.

Bubbles scudded, popping to the surface of his Guaraná. I still couldn't believe he wasn't just drinking water and hitting himself with a hammer or something. He was in the full regalia, though, bare-chested and bare-shouldered under sweeps of silky orange cloth, with a papery-looking umbrella propped against his knee. Another belt of wind struck the plane and a few rows up an older woman went 'Uy' and laughed.

I watched the trolley ease towards our seat. I caught the eye of the guy pushing it, shook my glass with what must have been enough irony to get a giggle out of him, or else he and the other staff must have been in full-on placation mode. I held my glass out for another go of the bad Cab Sauv, watched it glug to the brim, had a big slug of it, felt my skull loosen, lighten, the bone turn to raggy skeins. At least that was real.

The monk said 'No, thanks' to a refill and I tinked what was left of a fingernail against the rim of his glass and said, 'Are you allowed to have that?'

He frowned at the fingertip and said, 'Not really.'

'Have I rumbled you?' I said, and shifted towards him in the chair, lowering my voice. 'Are you really a monk?'

He blanched and retreated and said, 'I was ordained in 1977.'

'Is it just that you're extremely Dutch? And it's just you like the colour? You can be honest.'

He looked down at his robe and plucked the folds of it and said, 'I do like the colour. But no.' He took a business card out of a fold in his robe: a golden-spoked wheel printed on ivory.

I took the card and sat back in the chair and said, 'Well, alright.' I whapped the card against my palm. 'No offence.'

'You can never be too sure,' he said.

'I hate planes,' I said and sighed.

'I think that take-off,' said the Dutch monk, 'is perhaps one of the most exhilarating human experiences available.'

'Yeah, because you feel as though you're about to die.' I ground the heel of my hand against my forehead. 'Which you can't say you aren't either, can you. Because when you're up there on a plane you're not anywhere; you're not in any time, either. You're between the time zone in one place and the time zone in the other. You're between the name of the place you've come from and the name of the place you're going to. You're nowhere. So, if the plane goes down and you die there, where did you die? When did you die? You just got pulped and twisted to a big twist of human jerky that you'd need machines to identify, big scared gob gaping on you showing all your teeth, and that's if your face makes it at all. And then where's your grave, if they don't get you back? Some dot of sea. Some dot of land. Some grassy nothing. Who the fuck knows. It's not dead, it's gone. As though nothing ever happened. Nobody's ever more dead than the cunts who die on a plane. And you're not even alive when you're on the plane, either, up there, because you haven't landed yet. You're Schrödinger's gobshite, aren't you? Dead and alive at the same time up in the air. Because they take off your belt and your shoes and your jacket and your bag and they lump you through the little security arch and out into the fucking shops and you don't fully resume your solidity until your plane lands and that's if you land. You die in that cram of the queue for a bit and maybe you come back and maybe you don't and what it gives me when I'm in an airport is an abattoir feeling, all that ringing shiny echoing fucking hallways going on and on and on, and they're all crammed with people who are neither dead nor alive. And it's impossible to think how many of us there all are and have been and how you have this only lonely tiny life and it's there in the middle of the cram. And that's shite, isn't it. If you're basically dead and reborn every time you get up all high and all and then come down again.'

The Dutch monk frowned and said, 'I think all deaths are basically this really though, aren't they. You know. Everything falling away from you all at once. Place. Name. Time. So, where's the problem?'

'The problem's you come back,' I said.

'I can't imagine anyone recovering from having fallen into this world.' The monk ran a hand over his scalp. He frowned a little. Then he shrugged and beamed. 'But what can you do.'

'Oh, I know what that's like,' I said, and now it was my turn to wag my finger at him. 'That's me the whole time like.'

'Since when?' said the monk.

9

'Oh, weeks.' I flapped a hand. Wine splashed. The sound of it amplified in my head into the crash of knocking my girlfriend's Elis Regina poster to the ground with a flung wine bottle the day she'd left. That hadn't been my first option for taking it down. I'd tried with a drill first, climbed a stepladder, slipped off, saw a flash of yellow light, then all the lights in the apartment died and even the hum of the fridge fell quiet. I'd hit the tile with a squawk, the drill still whizzing in my grip, sure that I'd electrocuted myself so suddenly that my soul hadn't realised I was dead, sure that the noise of the drill actually the mortician's saw opening my chest, while Elis Regina still hung by one screw from the wall, grinning and swinging above me, knowing I was dead, and I had cried for a while, then flung the wine bottle at the poster, and then at last it had crashed to the ground. I wasn't sure what day that had been, but, if I was dead, which I couldn't be sure I wasn't, then it wouldn't really matter. I walked around the apartment amid drifts of broken glass and sharded ceramic because I wasn't arsed washing anything, I just threw the plates and glasses either at my girlfriend's cat or at the walls. Sometimes I'd pick up the pieces and cut my forearms with them for a while.

'But, you see,' the Dutch monk said, 'those afterwards spaces, they are the same space as the before spaces. I don't think we ever really leave this place.'

'Really?'

'No, no,' he said. 'Once you fall in here it's sort of not possible to recover, I think. Even if you disperse, you disperse inside space, don't you. It's all matter.'

He lifted the soda to his lips. 'It's all bardo time, how-ever you look at it.'

'Right.' I pushed a sweat-wet lock of hair off my forehead. 'Bardo time.'

He squinted a little and had his hands resting on his thigh. Bubbles still popped in the dregs of his Guaraná, but fewer of them now. Time had definitely passed. He made a crease of his mouth and he nodded and he said, 'It's not an easy place, Brazil.'

'It isn't,' I said, suddenly unsure again if I'd been talking or silent or if he could just read my thoughts.

But then there was a deep electronic ting overhead and the seatbelt sign went on. I saw flight staff go leg-ging it up the aisle. The intercom crackled and the har-ried pilot said something about an all clear for take-off and cheers – some sarcastic, most relieved – went up from the passengers.

'Oh, good,' said the monk, and took a last drink of Guaraná and flexed and relaxed his hands on the rests. 'I think I'll meditate a little.'

'Enjoy,' I said and toasted him with the wine, and then he shut his eyes and I wiped whitish dehydration goop from my lips and watched the warm gone smile spread across his face. How did he get to that place in himself so fast, so easily? There must have been no buzz-ing in his head, no wires sticking out of his thoughts, no leaky pipes gurgling over the top of whatever words he tried to find. I eased myself back in my seat. My hands gripped the armrests hard. The storm scraubed and pressed the glass, the curved ceiling, the walls. The plane might burst, I thought, or else my skull might.

My hands rose unbidden to the top of my head and I leaned forward, clutching my hands crosswise over the top of my skull, trying to hold the bone plates under my skin together. My fingers slipped, regripped. Those bone plates couldn't come apart. If they did the memories would come, seeping up all black and corrosive, eating holes in things, holes wide enough for me to fall down out through. I rocked in my seat. It didn't work. The memories were coming. The black pool was rising. I had never really left. I could never really leave. It would always be in me, an underground lake slopping back and forth, back and forth, black as obsidian, and as cold, with a deep mineral blood-and-sulphur smell breathing off it, like a million blocked drains. And all I could do was succumb.

When it comes to Ireland, I probably need to start with the shit.

In the third or fourth year of my drinking, while I was still an undergraduate, I began to lose control of my bowels. This would announce itself with a sudden lava heat and a prickling of dread across my nape, as my guts liquefied and I had to scarper to the nearest toilet. That melting sensation could hit just about any time: at a house party, on a first date, in class, at a book fair, in a farmers' market. If I was lucky, I'd feel the melt in time and make it to the jacks with only my jocks ruined. It was horrible – a long greenish-black scarf, the shit of a cormorant. When I was not lucky, the first I'd know of it would be the heat and the sudden cooling on my ass-cheeks, and off I'd have to go, no matter where I was.

A lot of the time I was on my own. When I wasn't, I got very good at keeping a poker face, receiving a fake text, and fleeing. I have no idea how effective these performances were.

One Sunday, some friends of my flatmate's were over visiting. I came in drunk and high from the night before and got everyone a drink. Then I shat myself, sprang to my feet and jokingly said I was off to pass out. I got into the shower fully clothed. I could hear everyone laughing. I put the shower on full blast and scoured the green stain out of the seat of my pants, the pressure up so high it fizzed against the fabric, the suds foaming up white through the black of my jeans.

I began to calculate my movements in terms of the likelihood that I would shit myself on a given outing. I'd take bigger risks when it was something important, such as buying wine. I can remember these sorties only from the outside, as though watching myself on CCTV: my hair everywhere, my body narrow as a number one, a hunch to my shoulders, a face on me like a sad cartoon cat with glasses on. I'd listen to the gargle of my stomach and press a hand to it, checking if it was hunger or the telltale downward chundering sensation. House parties were OK. Pubs were difficult, but manageable. Classes were almost impossible. Still, though, I went, even if it meant filling my reusable coffee cup with crap wine in order to get through them without my body shivering me from the chair.

It had to be wine: it was the easiest thing to drink on an empty stomach, and drinking on an empty stomach was important, too, because when I woke up I needed a big slug or I would go straight into a panic attack. Wine was economical, getting you pissed at a slow but steady pace, faster than beer, but not as fast as heavier spirits, where you'd wind up feeling the whole time as though your hands were trembling on the steering wheel of your drunkenness's speeding F1 car. I would put away three bottles a day; the first taking me through to afternoon, then requiring a bit of soakage to prevent that acid-reflux heart-attack feeling. The second would smooth into the buzz of the first, a kind of golden cruise that allowed me to get work done, topped up now and then with vodka-spiked coffees until the jitters became untenable and I had to tip in bottle three. This shut me down for the night: a gesture equivalent to scudding water over a laptop because the fan's gone too loud.

One lecturer told me I had a tendency to answer everything but the question. I'd quite fancied that idea of splatter patterns of information pocking the white of the page, eventually shaping out something that couldn't be expressed, but in retrospect I think the lack of focus probably ought to have struck me as a symptom of illness rather than an omen of greatness. I worked through it all the same, pushed it under, got on with it.

*

Concealment has always been my preferred relationship with pain. I can't remember when I first wanted to kill myself. This is to say that I can't remember a time when I didn't want to kill myself. Trying to reach back to a time before that need peels my fingers apart from within, I reach towards the keyboard and I hear the shrilling of girders bending away from one another, the metal coming away strip by strip. It's not as if I don't have happy childhood memories. It's not as if anybody died – a parent, I mean, or a sibling. Nothing burst a hole in the home around me. Maybe nothing needed to. Maybe it just never felt solid.

There was a time when my father worked in England during the week because it looked like we might lose our house. While he was gone my mother didn't find it so easy. I remember her getting upset when I brought back an apple from school uneaten. I don't remember why I couldn't eat at school: the food seemed to cool, lose its sheen, become a gross puck of matter on its trajectory from home to class, and to wedge down bite after bite that clagged in my teeth felt as if I was stuffing my gizzard with fibreglass or damp wood. But I couldn't tell her this. To tell her this would be too much for her.

But this all feels like a big deal over nothing. There has to be something more, something worse, something that explains everything. When I try to think of what's under this, the food and the panic, I get no further than the image of a panel or pane of flesh, lit from above, so that the pane glows red-brown, almost as if lit from within, and flayed, flayed across, up, down, diagonally, curls and frays of whipped grey ex-flesh clinging to the gouges across the centre. The mass of scarring is illegible, but the colours shift in tone the closer or further away I get: yellow-red tints, brown of dried blood, that warm, warm brown. Nothing is legible here. I talk into the scarring and the flesh mass drinks all sound. I could punch it but all I'd feel was a flat deadening wobble of non-resistance – just this rubbery unechoing thud back at me.

Sometimes I want to push my head through this stretched reddish hide as far as I can. I want to know if all the pain I talk about is an exaggeration produced by my thinking and my words and my identifying with other people's stories. Sometimes in that image the whitish fat within stretches ectoplasmic around my skull till

I smother inside. Other times there's a pop and I burst through and what I find there is a screaming black zone, where numbers that aren't numbers and words that aren't words and voices that aren't voices go whipping past my head in a razor-edged cyclone, shaving the skin off me, working the skull until it, too, bursts, a glitter-cloud of blood, brainfoam, bone, afloat in the void. I might call that the truth, if there was one.

*

I recall a strained, irritable atmosphere at home, my sister and I forever ready to bite at each other. I don't remember what we were afraid of: I don't think of our parents. I think we were just afraid of whatever our parents were afraid of, and that was illegible to me. My sister had asthma. I remember one attack, bad enough for her to die of; she must have been six, I must have been eight; the pink glow of light in her room, the burn sound of her breath going in and out, on and on, enough for me to feel the scorch of it in my chest, too, lying there beside her, desperate to sleep, unable to sleep, sure that if I slept she'd die. My own sicknesses must have been in my mind, I suppose. I don't remember anything wrong with my body – an allergic reaction once that left me scrawled all over with red mottling, but only for a day; a fall down a stairs that didn't even break my arm. I used to eat crayons and pencils – black, yellow, brown, trying to stew up a glopid and bitter soup in my stomach, enough to burn the walls, enough to turn my shit to something monstrous. Even

17

now I dream about sicking up lengths of graphite, the foam of bubbles around each chunk bursting, popping, sizzling, the acid of my gut leaving them nubbled and pitted. When I wake up from these dreams I'm empty, peaceful, released. But in real life nobody picked up on any oddity in my behaviour.

They had enough going on, I suppose, my parents. I recall my father saying *You're right, you're right, I'm wrong* or *I'm sorry, I'm sorry* about things he did wrong, but in a tone of rushed urgency that suggested these words were a synonym for *Leave me be, Leave me alone.*

He's not like that anymore, though. He's written a lot down and shared it with me and others. I seem to recall a long poem, with end-stopped lines, armoured containers for beloved sensory data: riverwater heaping blackly past, galaxy swirls of ox-eye daisies and sowthistle and vetch in grass so deep it holds your body's imprint for a moment as you pass through it, so thick you could let yourself fall, be borne up by it. Strong-haunched rabbits heel up their tails, vanish under a shine-seam of wire. There's a children's novel my father wrote when two of my cousins were in hospital, in part to entertain them, which featured long chains of unpiloted robots bombing down upon the despised home of the villains, who were mistreating animals (they weren't home; nobody died). But there were darker patterns in the writing.

He was pulled away from home by a scholarship to a boarding school on whose construction his father worked as foreman. His father said, *I think you'll find it won't be so different from home. And,* my father said to me, *he wasn't wrong.*

How hard my father tried to publish his writing, if he did at all, I have no idea; I think the act of finding words and laying them down was enough. His posture was often softened by hours in the study. I saw the hunted, haunted look go from his eyes. I saw his forehead uncorrugate. He ate more slowly. He played more pool. He saw his friends more. Our house became busy: his friends, my ma's friends. He'd found the words and they'd taken something from him. He was breathing freely. He wrote it all out of him, whatever *it* may have been. He didn't go back to it. He built a boat instead. He milled the strips, caulked the joins. He bent the stems. He shut the hulls. He sanded along the gunnels and the keel and the inner curves till all was one single smooth piece. *For low water only,* he told me: the Barrow, the Greese – waterways of his childhood, waterways of his poem. We'll go in it together him and my ma and me. We'll smooth past the old houses and old streets and they'll hover as far as the bank and encroach no further. The shapes will flip and lose solidity in the surface that heaps past, gallon upon gallon, never the same river one second to the next, everything leaving itself behind, all the time. The prow will nudge through spreading zeroes of foam passing the outdoor public swimming pool my ma used to go to when she was a kid: lichen rosettes on old concrete, ivy crampons, their spreading black nervature. She never stopped swimming all her life. I learned from her, followed the gloss and heave of her strong shoulders pushing against the deep suasion and pushback of the waves she pushed up with every stroke, her breath pistoning, steady, sure, eyes front, blank with concentration: or else the opposite of blank, and maybe just concentrated, the way a bird of prey looks right before the swoop. My swim's upwards, out from in, not across, not like hers – a lake, an impossible lake, greeny-black, ink runoff from all my heaped-up pages; up from beneath, via glooms lit by anglerfish, gross salpy shapes slicking cool across my skin.

What I'd give to burst the surface, fling back the head, hear droplets spatter in fantails out behind me, too relieved even to gasp, the chest-crush and the forceps-crush on my temples lifted away. The metaphors will seem tired to you. Tired writers seep tired writing. The fatigue and disgust. But even then, even on the surface, the sentences still fly at me in swarms between midnight and three in the morning. They buzz my head. They strafe my skin. They make me flail like an ape. When I give up and lie down they beat me to death, beat me into peace, I hope, but they never hit hard enough.

*

But we're not there yet. We're still under. Clumps of memory bloom up still, caught trash finding an air-pocket, bumping me in the dark. It's my grandfather now, the last time I saw him, a jaundiced spindle of himself in a hospital bed at Waterford Regional, trying to remember my age, trying to talk to me, in that sad gentle voice he had. He was never bad to me. There's a picture of me sitting on his knee showing him the book

I was reading, a glass of 7Up sizzling at his elbow, and simply by thinking I can bring back not just that picture but his smell of denim and metal shavings. I know I was thinking about that picture when I was looking at him in the hospital bed, because there wasn't much else to think about at such times; and, if I didn't, then the only memory I'd take away from that hospital – that cheesecake-coloured light, that click and buzz of the machines keeping him alive – would be the way my own father was sitting on the chair across from the bed, his elbows on his knees, his body leaning forward, his stare utterly blank, but seeming to come from a long way back in his head, looking at his father in a way I swore I would never look at mine. I'd fix whatever was off or bad in me that would make me see my father that way. I promised myself I would.

*

It's been said that all mothers are single mothers regardless of marital status: that's how I felt about my mother for those years. She'd queue up to buy VHSes so she could tape the cartoons for my sister and me, under these horrible Kilkenny afternoons where the buildings and the clouds are the same tint and weight, where the rain seeps down, tinfoil-coloured. She'd do that even when she'd rather have been anywhere else. But she wanted to keep us wrapped in that pod of happy pictures and electric light and safe noises, so she put herself out there. I'd trip out when she panicked, see things that weren't there: a man who'd fly low overhead carried by a broken umbrella, his old-Brillo-pad hair and beard on him, laughing to himself as he glided over the town. An image comes to me here of my earliest wakings – the routine ones, the ones unmarked by something special, different to the time I sat up and saw a column of plastic dinosaurs marching from the crack of light falling through my bedroom door, one after the other, in a shapely S all the way to the foot of my bed, perhaps as many as eleven, twelve of them, diplodocus, dimetrodon, tyrannosaurus rex, stegosaurus, ankylosaurus, plesiosaurus – an image of purple banks of cloud, dark hills and a golden weather-vane spinning like a propeller. I turn my head and see the rucked covers of my mother's bed. She's up. I can stay in bed for more time. On days when I wake up too early it's as if I'm back there again, rolling in the shallows of sleep, still warm, somehow, those parts of me still covered by sleep, covered by the smell of my mother's warm body, milky skin smell, fabric softener, toothpaste. The radio burbles low, puts out names: Netanyahu and Arafat, Clinton and Mary Robinson, the stories not quite clear enough for me to make out what they're about: the language tumbles on and on, a black river of talk with a shine of light on it.

These pictures sound calm, comforting, but there is a balled-up fear rolling around behind my ribcage. I do not want to be away from this body even though this body tells me terrible things sometimes, but the day is about to rip me away from this body all the same. I can't figure out who put the fear in my body or how to get it out, and I don't even know what it's about – my mother's moods, my father's moods, my sister's moods, the kids at school, the gritty squeak of shoes on muck-tracked lino, the grittier squeak of chalk on the black-board, the way I don't ever, ever get enough time to hide from all of that in the spread-out cushions of the library corner, drinking cool air through the gap in the prefab wall, trying to make the view of grey sky or blue air and green plants seem to frame somewhere else other than where I've had to wake up yet again.

I think I never felt safe around my mother. I don't mean that she was a danger: I mean that she was *in* danger. She never seemed steady on her own. I seem to remember her shouting one day – not at my sister exactly, or even about her, so much as over something she seemed to feel that *she* might get in trouble for – but I remember my sister crying, face red and scrunched up in a way that honestly annoyed me, but that I could only sympathise with, since my own face had that look more times a week than I would ever want to admit to myself or in front of anyone.

I'd found a book on my mother's dresser, the indigo cover showing a chalk outline of a curvy nude woman whose hair mapped the shapes of her hips. This book said that sometimes it was necessary for a mother to rest. So I said to my sister, trying to reassure her, *Don't worry: it's not your fault; Mam just needs a rest.* The shouting stopped. My mother's jaw snapped shut and she looked at me like I'd slapped her.

I can't remember what happened next.

*

Another memory rises now. When exactly this happened, I've no clue, but I remember being alone with my mother and sister at my grandfather's house and suddenly hearing my mother come legging it down the stairs, wailing. For a second I couldn't move. I wanted to think I was imagining it. But then the noise didn't stop, the freeze of realisation spread in my gut, and I let the ball I'd been playing with drop and went running out to her, the commentary from the game still yattering away in the sitting room behind me. There she was, sitting on the mealy red strip of carpet that went up the middle of the stairs, under the framed pictures of the dogs playing poker that Grandad had hung there, sobbing into her knees. When she heard me ask her if she was OK she looked up with these huge eyes as though she'd no idea who I was, or how she and I had come to be there at the same time, and then I saw the recognition wash through her, and she put her face between her hands, and all I heard was her saying, 'Oh, God, I'm so sorry, I really am.' I'd never seen a face look that naked before. On the way home, either later that night or the night after, I remember the dark huge around the train, the tiny cold latticework of orange lights on the hills, a Virgin Mary in a greenish lit-up vertical box outside a cemetery – upright coffin, glass crawled all over with vapour inside. And I remember a moss-coated, stony-solid feeling sliding down my gullet from just looking at the world through the window, in all its coldness.

When these pictures come, they replay themselves. They go on and on, but they also seem very short. They loop, but they don't repeat: or else they repeat, but don't loop: who knows what the difference is, they go on for ever, they last for seconds, they go around for ever, I can't tell with what moment they begin, with what moment they end, they start in the middle, they reach back, they go forwards, they start again, when I feel they're about to continue on from the usual ending point they don't, because they don't link to anything, they're whirlpools, they pull me in, they pull me down, they spit me out miles from where I began, lapped in dirt-grey billows, face up, too exhausted to swim. When the pictures go still, sometimes one image hovers, and seems to burn itself into my brain. I can smell the singeing. I don't want to remember them. They remember me. They visit me. They are demons pulling at my limbs. I hate the pictures. I know I talk about coals a lot: a body stuffed with hot coals, piled up and up in a pyramid inside, a magmatic glow pulsating beneath the nested black eggs of the coals stuffing my throat. I come back to that image because it's the same place and sensation that I get sent to every time. That throat, those coals, those pictures, always waiting to push through the skin of memory and make themselves visible. Writing is me chucking the coals off the furnace so my thoughts don't chuck more on.

*

Suicide is the one thing I have ever wanted without any ambivalence. That's why I'll never do it. I'm never meant to do what I want. What I want wants to kill me. If I learned anything from all this fucking shite

I learned that. Even the word *suicide* was a taboo in my house. My father used to say that if he was found dead and it was said to be a suicide, that we should investigate, because he'd never do anything of the kind to us. All suicides were suicide bombings, leaving pain and bone shards stuck deep in everyone around for ever after, the way it had in the body of a lad in my class who came home one Wednesday to find his da'd hanged himself. I caress the image daily. When things were bad in secondary school, I would paint little black dots on my wrists, just below the cuff, and think to myself how all I had to do was press down on the black button with a knife point and it would all be over: my first sense of a magic button, of instant relief, the first of so many. Each ink dot was a little black pool, going a teal tint as the sweat of the day thinned out the pigment, the surface of that pool inside me, the consistency of molasses, heavy with mineral silt. All I had to do was wade in up to my thighs and the weight of the sediment would pull me down the rest of the way.

This, I think, was the knowledge that I would have to kill myself to get away from suffering, but also the knowledge that killing myself would bring even more suffering on the way out of the suffering, meaning that there was no relief from the suffering, not really, just water gulfing down my neck: then lungburn, dread, body pleading for this not to be the end. I can still hear that black pool sloshing. It's still there, still inside. It still waits.

One day in a fit of rage I revealed these feelings to someone who was bothering me at school. A concerned friend told the principal how I was getting on. I'm not sure I knew what I was saying even though I felt it very deeply. I'll never forget the look on my father's face walking into the office when I was summoned there too, to answer for these claims. I hadn't expected to see him there. When they came for me I'd assumed it would be about something else. I'd been leaving apples in my bag and bringing them home from school. They'd begun to ferment. A brown stain was showing through on the front of it. There was a rank cidery bang off of it. At school, people laughed at it. At home nobody noticed. Slinging the bag into the car at the end of the day brought no reaction. I couldn't understand it. The school must have told my family. I was nervous walking down the lino of the corridor, hearing my steps echo, behind the brisker steps of the guidance counsellor who'd come for me. I wasn't used to getting in trouble but I knew what it felt like and this was what it felt like – that floorless feeling in the stomach, all of me about to come apart, spill down into nothing, in a drumming of falling limbs, same as in those video games where you had to blow people up. I didn't want to be in trouble. Not being in trouble was the only thing I had to show for going to school, and I wasn't even able to manage that anymore. Now we were at the front office. The door opened. And there was my father, sitting there looking terrified, as though I'd died already. My guidance counsellor sat down. She started talking. She started to tell my father about the black dots on my wrists. I put my head down. I didn't want to see any of what came next.

'But he doesn't want to die,' stuttered my father. 'He likes. He likes so many things. He likes The Beatles.

He likes football. Liverpool. He watches James Bond films. He's. He's. Normal.' I watched my father pushing his lower lip into his mouth. Some membrane or other sagged inside my chest. I hadn't wanted this. I'd wanted something else. I'd wanted to be dead, sure, but not to kill myself: I'd wanted to just stop, if that was possible, I wanted to will my heart to a stop, discreetly cease, without the fuss and the blood. More than being dead, more than killing myself, I'd wanted to be made to feel safe.

I felt the guidance counsellor looking at me with a gaze that was nearly angry, nearly suspicious, like I was lying, like I'd said something she might catch; like I'd coughed in her face, maybe, I don't know. And now she had to wipe it off her, make what she'd heard sound like a lie to herself. There was nothing for me here.

I can't recall how I talked them down, made them not worry. I think I started talking about the outer ring of my fears, the stuff that sounded stupid to me even when I thought about it. This was enough to make them laugh – the guidance counsellor with relief, my father with a kind of sadness around the edges. Before I knew it, I had trivialised what was making me so upset, while leaving the core of the pain unnoticed. Driving home, my father became relieved enough to feel angry at me. When we got home he grabbed my wrists and shook his head at the points where the black spots were. I let myself go blank, limp, biddable, as though in a pair of powerful jaws, inert in the great jets of his fearful angry talking: and I slumped there apologising, saying I was exaggerating, lying, playing a game to get people to take me seriously. I still don't know if that's fully untrue. That, I think, is maybe the worst thing about all of it.

*

One Christmas, years later, when I was just over a year off the muck, I was on assignment in a part of Chihuahua where Mexican journalists were often killed for their stories. I was covering a story for Al Jazeera about gangs kidnapping gifted endurance runners from the Rarámuri community and making them cross the US border with backpacks full of the heroin and fentanyl that was in its turn driving the long-term marijuana farmers in the area out of business. The old 'foreigner-slash-correspondent protective shield' was not so durable up in that neck of the woods as it was elsewhere: Miroslava Breach, a Mexican investigative journalist who reported on organised crime and drug trafficking – and who was a colleague to many of my friends – had been murdered outside her home in Chihuahua not long before, in March 2017; soon after we left, a teacher from the US was executed for befriending too many interesting people and asking them too many interesting questions.

My friend, Lalo, came with me as a photographer. On our last night, out too late, we pulled up at our hotel. A big red pickup was parked outside. We looked at each other. We knew the kind. You could hear what kind: a brass-led narcocorrido was bumping out of the speakers, El Komander or Valentín Elizalde or some other one of those objectionable fucking cunts who I despise. The front door opened. Out got a young, clean-shaven guy wearing a padded red Ralph Lauren Polo gilet over a Tommy Hilfiger shirt. He waved and beamed. The other three men in the car – interchangeable hefty lads, flat-top baseball caps, eyes blank as river pebbles – did not wave. And I remember thinking in that moment that shitting myself or pissing myself or begging or panicking was not going to make this moment any better, so why do it, why not try to remain calm, take a last look at the coiling fog, the dark blue air, the cobbled streets, try to make it look the way Kilkenny looked, and breathe through whatever had to be breathed through: go limp, go pliant, go biddable, because whatever they'd decided to do, they'd decided a while ago.

'Now what the fuck might you two be doing up around here?' laughed the red gilet guy as he clapped me on the shoulder.

'Sports journalists,' I said, and I tried to imitate the big friendly beam on him. The beaming was easy: it wasn't fully a lie. Inside in the car the interchangeable hefty lad in the passenger seat had his eyes on me. Above him, above the roof of the pickup, clouds were smoking downwards over the mountains: rain falling someplace.

'I love sports,' said Gilet Guy. 'What sports you like?'

'I like football,' I said. 'Liverpool.' I swallowed. 'You?'

'Oh, I'm a big wrestling guy, me,' said the red gilet guy. He gave a backward nod at Lalo, who had his hands crossed over his camera bag. 'What about your friend?'

'My friend's a man of culture,' I said.

The red gilet guy's face suddenly hardened and he said, 'You like wrestling?'

I'd been once, with my da and an ex whose soft manner had converted into something demonic on contact with the spectacle of men in spandex leathering the shit out of each other. We'd enjoyed watching the transformation in her more than we had the men in spandex. I couldn't remember shit about the ring itself. I had nothing. But then something floated up from those long grey evenings high up in the library: Roland Barthes, writing about lucha libre.

'Yeah, wrestling's cool, man,' I said. 'Yeah. The rudo and the técnico. The rough guy and the precision guy. Good and evil. The eagle and the serpent. Could you get any more Mexican?'

Lalo goggled at me. Gilet Guy squinted at me, and then he said, 'You want to know what I do?'

I remembered my father's gaze on me the day he'd taken me home from school with the black dots still on my wrists. I remembered that pliancy in me, trying to get the teeth of the afternoon to pass over me. I tried to call it up again, tried to let my body go as cool and pliant as I could without falling down. I kept a warm numb smile on my face. Every breath going in and out of my nose had that chlorinated taste of fear off of it. If they were quick about it, I didn't think I'd mind what happened. The trouble, of course, is that they weren't ever that quick about it. They were bullies, as bad as the lads in school. They wanted tears, then blood, then nothing. But somehow it was all less scary than that afternoon with my father. All I had was a slight tingling along the floor of my stomach. Even that would be over before long. Inside the jeep the song ended and another song that sounded exactly the same as the previous song started. I hate narcocorridos.

'What you do?' I said. 'You want me to ask you what you do?'

The guy's squint deepened to a frown.

'Yes,' he said. 'What do you think?'

The guy in the passenger seat leaned around. The red gilet guy gave him a wink and raised a staying hand. I can't explain what I felt then: elation, heat, delight, the kind that doesn't care if it spatters to nothing in a mess of blood drops. This was way less bad than that afternoon with my dad. The system worked. You practise enough at being scared shitless of yourself and your loved ones all the time and eventually strangers who can actually do shit to you can't do shit to you.

'Tourism,' I said. 'You work in tourism.'

I saw Lalo close his eyes and shake his head.

The guy's frown turned to a glower – and then it broke. He beamed again, wagged a finger at us, said, 'You know what, man, I like you. You two are alright. You two go have a nice evening now. Get in out of this cold, right?' He gave a happy bark of a laugh and I shut my eyes for a second, an extra-long blink, opened them up, tried to look normal, tried to smile. Jesus Christ, I hated these people.

The red gilet guy gave a little salute. The men in the car did not. He closed the door. The jeep started, pulled off, still blaring El Komander or whatever the fuck other narcocorrido bollocks they got off on, the freaks, the imbeciles, the pillocks, the benighted fucking cunts. I watched the bluish vapour of the jeep's exhaust blur into the fog blanketing the streets.

Lalo turned his body to watch them disappear around the corner and out onto the road leaving town. Then he turned and said, 'Tourism's a good guess.'

'Why's that?' The fear or the elation or the uplift or whatever word you want to use for that weird, delighted panic, that feeling, it was going drumdrumdrum in me, making a speedbag of my heart; exaltation, let's call it exhilaration – I don't know, any of those words that mean you're lifted out of yourself.

'Yeah,' Lalo muttered and kicked a pebble. 'This here's a magic town.'

'Yeah?'

'Yeah,' he said. ''Cause you come here, you disappear.'

'Were you scared?' I said.

'What do you think?'

I shrugged, said, 'Yeah?'

'Fuck yeah I was scared,' he said. 'Were you?'

I shrugged. 'You can't kill what's already dead,' I joked in a deep, gravelly action hero voice, because even though I wasn't joking the only way to say what I was getting at was to make a joke out of it – I'd only come to life inside when the fear had hit me, up to then I was zombieing along, way I had been for as long as I'd been off drugs and maybe for as long as I'd been on them, too.

Lalo swatted the air with his hand and clicked his tongue, cocking his head back in disdain, then he said he'd found a place on the Happy Cow app that had vegan options like setas al ajillo and that we should go maybe try it before it closed for the night. My head was ringing. I couldn't hear my own voice too well, and his *Sounds good* reached me from an underwater distance. I walked through the dark with him, the orb lamps on the square pulsing on their posts, thinking how I still hadn't been as scared talking to those guys in the jeep as I had been of my father that afternoon. Turns out, it had been the perfect training.

*

As for the pain itself, the stuff I'd been trying to keep from my father and the guidance counsellor, I've no idea where it came from. It's not as though I hated school, or even my town. And it's not as though I didn't have friends, either: we used to pretend we'd debating practice, then skive off, go hurtling down the back streets, go steal an extra few minutes with our girlfriends somewhere nearer their school, try and sometimes succeed to buy proper cigarettes rather than rollies nabbed from older kids, that kind of thing. The schoolyard was sectored by year, so for around two years at the eleven o'clock breaks we used to chuck fruit and piss balloons at the other sectors and never got caught. In my last year at school, I had to do the valedictorian speech – or whatever we called it – and my first, indeed only, concern was working in a bit about the piss balloon ambushes. That got a standing ovation led by the piss balloon mastermind. I couldn't finish the speech. That's the only reason I feel proud of it. It was the same with debating: it was an excuse for jokes, preferably scabrous ones, and I didn't care if I lost as long as I got a laugh.

As well as that, Kilkenny's not ugly, only grim: long passageways smooth as throatlinings, a bluish lead shine to the stones of the buildings and the older streets, gargling with rain noise and footsteps on wet days. Days like those I used to find a perch that looked out on those passageways, checked tiles underfoot, black and white photos of New York on the walls, coffee steam and chip heat thick around me, dreaming of elsewheres that always somehow looked the same as the town I was sitting in: redbrick townhouses, amber windows high up under frowning eaves, rich with the kind of promise their interiors could never match – yes, the same town, just slightly shifted, slightly angled, so that the sharp trash stuck inside me didn't show.

I remembered reading the myth of Androcles and the lion, about how people who hurt others are often hurting themselves, one day, lying on the ground, while at least three other kids kicked the shit out of me. I remember one kick going so hard right into my hole as I lay on the ground that I felt something happen in my guts, a tight bursting pain behind my navel. I stayed silent. I remember thinking that the white flash of pain that made me feel ill when it went through my head was almost something I could if not enjoy then at least perceive in its fullness rather than merely react to. If I could stay above the pain and try to think how he didn't know what he'd done then I'd be alright, then it'd be alright.

But I also remember being quite young and hearing my mother tell me about the library she'd gone to, next door to the house, the McGrath Hall, and telling me about the smell of the books, the click of the date stamp. *If I had that stamp*, she told me, *I could abolish time. I wanted that stamp*. She took me to the library and I loved it as well – the quiet under those high ceilings, rumbling with an undersong of words, thoughts, feelings, lives all around me. The place had a tin roof, and it turned the rain to a heaving ocean. That was my favourite sound. When everyone had gone to bed at night I'd tune the radio to in between stations to hear that white noise gust blowing, reading under the covers with a torch that came free in the *Beano*, the battery banjaxed, so I'd had to fold it to get the contacts to touch. In my little dim cave of light lost to rain noise there was no time. I was in the library, I wasn't at home. There was rain noise, there was book smell, my breath falling into time with the rhythm of imagined rain – that deep, amniotic slosh.

Stories, then, pulled me away from the world, high into my own head, away from the body. I was saying goodbye to it all. This wasn't entertainment: this was asceticism. I'd think of the martyrs I'd read about and seen pictures of in my mother's art history books and encyclopaedias at home, damaged into pure knowledge, pure equanimity: John of Patmos having the oil ladled on, Lawrence asking for the Roman soldiers to flip him over on the griddle, Lucia holding her own eyes on a plate, Bartholomew in Michelangelo's Sistine Chapel fresco, frowning in glum contemplation of the shreds of his earthly pelt, still not fully over it.

*

Around the age of fifteen, I began punishing my body with laxatives and emetic quantities of salted water. The impulse maybe had to do with not feeling worthy of the food I was given by my parents, I think, or else some more complex rejection, based on the sense I've always had that the love I received was conditional on good behaviour. That sense is everywhere, even now, a buzz of uncertainty and fear that runs around the outline of every interaction I have, however innocuous, however brief, deepening the shadow of that outline into a dread of punishment.

Nobody seemed to notice. There was one chest-tightening moment when my mother and father returned from a dinner party at their friends' house and queried the scrim of dried Andrews Liver Salts and water on the draining-board. I hadn't been able to say anything much, and they were too tired to press any further, I suppose. Discretion was important. I knew too many self-harming friends who'd been caught because they'd cut too hard or too often. I'd take a tube of toothpaste and, using the sharp corners at the bottom of the tube, draw long red exclamation marks from my wrists to the soft inner fold of my elbow. These faded quickly, but hurt like fuck, and the blinding white incandescence of it stilled the noise for long enough that I could breathe. There were other practices: twisting my own pubes until the skin lifted, red, around the base of each hair, then holding this for as long as I could; stabbing the backs of my hands with darts; going at the soles of my feet with razor blades. To this day I can't buy a safety razor without being afraid of what I'll do with it.

I don't know where this fascination with self-punishment came from. It's not as though I was that religious. I remember a leaden Friday where the gloss of the pre-rain air is the same as the gleam of evening on the black leather of my grandfather's chair, the one that vibrates when you play with some switches set into the lacquer of its arms. My father has gone out to get the Friday evening Chinese – I get sweet and sour chicken, those deep-fried golden almost-balls, and I'm looking forward to them. I get off on the way the hunger rolls over in my belly and stings a little around the edges with each turn of the rumbles inside me. The radio is playing. The same serious voice as ever is talking and I'm not sure why I hear the words so clearly today. The words stand out hard in the air: I can nearly see the smoking holes the letters leave hanging in the air. The words go on and now they're talking about priests and children. The word *ferns* is there as well, and I enjoy that word, it's a cool green cowl I can curl under, smell rainwetted black earth and the pepper sting of soaked stems. It's a safe word to be under. My body is vibrating. Priests are meant to be good. If you don't go to Mass it's touch and go about whether or not you go to heaven. I have spent the summer reading saints' lives and feeling guilty about the distance between me and them. On the wall between a stained-glass image of George Best and the *Sgt. Pepper* sleeve hangs a pencil drawing my mother did of Blessed Oliver Plunkett, all flowing hair and serene bearded sadness. But the radio is talking about things priests did to children, things I'm not supposed to know about yet and am not sure how or why I know them – snatched bits of TV, maybe, or the books I leaf through when nobody is upstairs and I can get into my parents' bedroom, that sour note of the paper also the sourness of that knowledge, grownup odours, not straightforwardly nice or tasty or sweet or salty.

Now my father's key grits in the lock and the door opens with a rattle of metal against wood and glass and he's coming up the hall, and in my head I see the fried look of the chicken balls and the hunger in my stomach isn't hunger anymore. I'd rather not eat anything ever again. It's not right for me to eat something fried the colour of coffins, and that has a body inside, too, same as when you go into a church and think it's going to be quiet and empty and there's a coffin right there aglister on the silver trolley, and just like all the sad bodies the radio is talking about, because the dates mean that a lot of the people the voice is talking about must be dead by now. Oliver Plunkett's eyes are on me from the wall. He looks sad: he gets it, sure, he just doesn't know what to do about it. And I am thinking now that if food is bad, and if the church and its priests are bad, then what else is bad that people have been telling me is good, and what else is good that might be bad? But that thought breaks now because my father has carried the hot greasemapped weight of the takeaway to the table and he's saying, 'Hiya, Tim,' in his nice voice, his gentle voice, the one that sounds the way polished floors look and newsagents smell, the one I remember from when I was perhaps not yet two and he'd go around the alphabet letters that ran in a perfect fence around the top of my cot and we'd try a word for each letter, around and around until I fell asleep – that lettered cage around my sleep, that safe cage, with those angled shadows falling over me, those letters that helped me name the sensations, but then brought problems of their own, because you couldn't just name them; someone had to hear them, too – and, even if they did hear them, I'd still be using somebody else's words for my feelings, and who could hear those without hearing somebody else's voice howling through the middles of the letters, talking for me, over me. I am staring into space remembering the shadows of the letters tattooing my body when my hunger for the Chinese food wakes up and whips over inside and I don't quite forget it, but I can eat over the feeling in me. I can put something into me that will make that snarl go flat enough inside me that it will look as if nothing's wrong.

*

My father told this story about the lettered cage to two friends of mine, Jovi and Frank, in the kitchen of the house next to my friend Alejandro Zambra's. This is about nine months ago. Frank was showing me a section he loved from *The Use of Man* by Aleksandar Tišma: a whole life, accordioned into a single paragraph, leaping across miles and years in the space of three sentences. It impressed me, too, that sense of temporal suction, a wind pulling the letters, making them wobble on their stems, almost. Jovi asked my father if I'd always been that way, if I'd always loved reading that much, and he told the story about the cot. As he did, my stomach tightened into a fist, and my fist tightened around my glass of sparkling water. Outside, the air seethed with a louder version of the water in my glass. Jovi was impressed by how young I'd picked up a book; I embroidered this with a story of how when we'd had no money and my father had been in England my mother had taught painting on wood, and how I'd offer to read to the women taking her class if they walked past my door on their way back from the bathroom or whatever. Once a student of hers hadn't come back to class, my mother had gone up to investigate, and she'd found the missing student sitting at the end of my bed, while I read aloud to her from whatever silly thing I'd been trying to put myself to sleep with. I can't have been more than six; I suppose she must have been my mother's age at the time. I remember she'd seemed to like listening to me. This drew a laugh from Jovi and Frank and a bit from my da, too, but what I was feeling under it was a queasy wriggling in the gut, thinking about the words I'd learned, the feelings they'd named, the things, the events, how much bigger than my head and my body they'd been, especially at that age. They'd named something I couldn't live or hadn't lived. I stood there with my finger moving back and forth around the curve of the glass and I asked myself if anything I'd lived or felt had been really me, really real, really mine, or if it had just been a quotation, an imitation, an echo produced by the way language acts in the brain, making me think I had to live up to some narrative or other.

I remembered the bedroom where I must have read to my mother's student; I remembered that I hadn't always felt so comfortable there. One night, when my mother had been out playing tennis, I'd sat up all night crying with my father and not telling him why because

I was worried about frightening him with the fears I had swimming through my head – what would happen after he died, after my mother died, after we all died, if the world was going to end, if there was a God: fears too big for words. I sat clutching my knees to my elbows and looking out at the white cone of light cast over the grass square at the centre of the housing estate where we lived. I don't know if it was that night or another, but I remembered running out of that bedroom onto the red carpet and its white diamonds, howling, terrified, my heartbeat shaking in my chest, the nightmare I'd woken up from playing in my head, my parents running, their faces terrified as well: too terrified, in fact, for me to tell them what I had in my head, because what I had in my head was a dream of being in the back seat of a long purple car driven by somebody who wasn't either of my parents, a landscape of burned grass and blackened trees outside, the tarmac cracked, red-faced priests banging gongs by the side of the road, the sky darkening, the road winding, the fear in me growing enough to ask the driver where we were going, and the skin at the back of my neck rising and shivering, almost lifting fully off, as a kind of livid devil turned in the seat and told me, *You're dead and we're in hell.*

I remembered my mother holding me, but that I felt stiff and awkward in her arms, and staring out past her shoulders at the dark rectangle of the open bathroom door behind her, sure that something else was about to loom out of there. I remembered my breathing slowing and the look on my father's face, frowning down at me, not sure what to do with me. I remembered deciding not to find the words for what was happening in my head. I remembered that silence turning over, rolling tighter, a greyish wad of clay being folded in on itself, becoming a clench, a hardness. Nothing has unbunched it since.

When I have to write a scary scene for my fiction, I begin with some version of this: the trapped passenger, the weird road, the driver who suddenly turns out to be someone you can't trust. Even now, typing this, alone in a room, late at night, all the lights on, door locked, music on loud in case the upstairs neighbour opens a door or moves around and makes me jump out of my skin, I can feel the breath go in and out of my mouth and nose with an ethanol sting on it. The fear's vaporised the circulation of my blood and respiration into something hot and volatile. Who knows when I'll be without it. I think it might only finish when I do.

*

My father's impression, he said, was that too much progress retards, and so they were worried about the feelings and the words, the relationships between them. Did the words give me access to feelings that weren't mine – that I wasn't able for yet, that I hadn't lived, that I perhaps would never live, perhaps would never be able for? Did the words inside me somehow invent those feelings? Was there anything in me that wasn't a quotation of something greater, a mutation of that virus of language inside my little, individual system? The pictures they gave me, the places, the woodcuts of distant battles, the photographs of other worlds, other countries, other people – did they give me a greed for the toomuchness of it all, and no way to hold that feeling, that information, that excess? Were they ever really there? Was there a way to get to them that wasn't just me moving to a different place in words? And so: were the words to blame? Are the words the real temptation, with all their hidden riddles and exaggerations, tunnel systems that lead to nowhere in the darkness beneath the splits and ravines and canyons of a karst landscape? So, was it my vocabulary that did this to me?

I said none of this to my father. He said none of it to me. But the way he frowned and squinted in the light of the kitchen, hands on his hips, waiting in silence while our Uber slowed through the wet towards the door of Frank and Jovi's house, it made me think that we would maybe never get to the bottom of this. All I could see in my head was an oil painting by Rembrandt – the body of the ox, lit up gold, stub legs aiming up and out, and the obsidian glitter of the darkness beyond and around. I can imagine myself climbing out of that liquid, smoky darkness, which is the ink having run off every page I've ever blackened, as though coughed out, but the furthest I can get is to lie on the light that circles beneath the stubby legs and lopped neck of that hanging split-open trunk of meat in the Rembrandt. All I can do is lie there beached in the meat-smell of that light and shadow, contemplating the mutilation, hearing the creak of the ropes against the wood frame as the ox torso sways above me.

On my first day of Freshers' Week I approached the Literary Society stand, ready to foist my manuscript on the guy sitting there. He can still do a pretty good impression of this moment. He musses his hair, he hunches his posture, he lowers his voice to speak in a rapid, incomprehensible mumble, telling the imagined listener – himself – that he has a drawerful of stories, if he just take a moment to read them, that'd be great, yeah, he's just looking to get them published, just looking to get them off his hands, you know how it is, ha ha. I used to find the imitation or the mime or whatever you want to call it funny. I still sort of do. But I'd find it a lot funnier if those stories had appeared in print, if someone had done something with them, if only that was to reject them. I remember well the feeling I had in my body going up to that stand. I was so close to a relief from all the buzzing in my head. I'd transcribed all that buzzing onto the pages, the words, but I could still hear and feel it in my chest. I needed someone to reach in and collect those mealy greyed stacks and blow the mess off them, leave them clean and bearable enough for other people to want to be around them.

I saw the guy behind the desk seeing me. I was sure he could smell the pain and fear breathing out of my pores.

He was only two years older than me, but with his cord jacket and scarf and easy manner he came off as a real writer, the kind you see on book covers. He and I became friends, but I'm not sure that pure, unproblematic friendship ever really exists between writers, especially not in their twenties. It's half arms race, half a blind mammalian nuzzle seeking after warmth, all teeth and fur and snuffling. My flatmate, Rob, was a better laugh. He was studying Classics. He didn't think anything good had been written since Dante so he had no desire to write shit. We'd sit around in cravats and drink beer so cheap that we'd felt more expensive not to buy it, without quite knowing how that was meant to make sense, and we'd try to find better ways of translating Catullus: *I saw your missus wanking off the magnanimous sons of Rome* was about as good as it got, unfortunately. We'd watch Christopher Marlowe documentaries, hoping to figure out if that portrait of him in a golden doublet above the motto *What feeds me kills me* was really him. I'd puff out zeroes of weedsmoke and talk about how in Greek *pharmakon* meant both *poison* and *cure*, which meant that alcohol and all the rest of it was actually good, it was actually burning you into a state of despair where you could really see what the problem was. Rob agreed and zoomed in the laptop screen on an image of a cherub holding an upside-down torch that was still somehow burning. *Quod me nutrit me destruit,* he said, rapped the screen and said, *That's a colloquial version of an older one. Quod me alit me extinguit.* I said, *What keeps me lit puts me out,* my voice all cottony with weedsmoke, and Rob said, *Or what drives me mad keeps me together, some shit like that, maybe*, and took the joint from my fingers.

*

I developed a fetish towards a kind of writing that wanted to destroy the reader. Yes, the point was to give everything, to drain yourself out, to invite all comers to have a suck on your carotid artery; and yes, the point within that was to feel as though you still hadn't done enough. I remember my first exposure to Lacan came in October of 2007, about two weeks before turning nineteen, during what was a particularly leaden autumn of lectures given by a beloved lecturer of mine in Trinity College, Dublin. He spent eight weeks using Sartre, Beckett and Kristeva to delve into Lacan's first six seminars. One week was particularly difficult. I couldn't get my head around what I had heard. My skull felt about to split along its horizontal curve on both sides trying to fit the information into the bone, which I imagined as peeling away in long ivory shavings under the force of the lecturer's thought. I asked him after class if there was something else I should read to get my head around what he'd just said, and he said, 'All of Beckett.' I told him that this was fine, because I'd already started doing that, and then he left quickly, and I felt as though I had detained him inappropriately. I think that the sticky guilt-spatter over this last part of the interaction is what made me detour via HMV on Grafton Street, buy the Manic Street Preachers' first album, look at the flaming EU flag on the back, and go home dizzy, by tram, to my sterile efficiency apartment in the student residence. The greasy weight of the purchase in my stomach made me not want to listen to the album all the way through. Even though *Generation Terrorists* was only sixteen years old by that point it felt as though it came from a time when there were different rules and more solidity. While I listened, my thumbnail scraped against the pillowcase behind my head, the rhythm of it a dry ragged trochaic panting of fear that went short-long, short-long, short-long. The lecturer had talked about the horrible ways our society handles birth. You are spat into a tiled, too-loud glare, surrounded by machines and the first hands you feel are those of gloved strangers. The gap between emergence via cleaning-up to mother's arms, that handful of seconds, it must last an eternity. He said everything is an attempt to make it seem as though that moment had never happened. Everything is always a botched reconstruction of that first moment of relief. It can never be that good again, because that first moment of things being good again is in turn a botched reconstruction of when you weren't even here. He talked about the muffled choral wash of sounds through a parent's stomach walls and into the womb as a sea-ache pulsing at the heart of particularly charged sentences or sequences of sentences in Proust, Beckett and Joyce.

The seminar room's lights had that mosquito buzz to them: the sound of it flared and dimmed, flared and dimmed, hot in my head. The lecturer's voice seemed to redouble, catch the thinnest of echoes, as though echoing from inside a porch. He appeared to digress or else I fell into a dream of some kind.

'What I tell you is alarming,' he said, and bobbed his head, his lips pursed. 'I don't deny this. I won't deny it's

48

difficult to get across.' He shrugged, raised his hands in concession, and gave a little laugh. 'As such, I must give you an alarmingly specific example, by means of illustration.' He frowned, his eyes raking the classroom, and his eyebrows turned owlish. 'I had a student once whose mother died when she was young. His father's response was to bring his sons into business with him: these sons, her brothers. The business failed. It opened up a great whirlpool of debt beneath them all. None were saved. One had a liver transplant. Another fled. The third became a psychoanalyst.' He coughed out a laugh. Nobody joined in. 'He was the most bunched of all. But his sister, my student, was desperate to become a mother. It was the only job that she'd ever wanted. But that her body wouldn't allow it: the economic chaos in the family business, the brother who'd pinball in and out of rehab before shooting off into dive bars and the entourage of his adored childhood hero George Best, the illness and death of another brother's wife – her own best friend – the interminable mourning she felt for her mother. She had miscarriages. When a pregnancy finally held to term, she was so desperate to just force this little being into life that she buckled her back out of shape for ever.' His eyes moved over the room again. 'She had gotten the only job she'd ever wanted, but appeared to spend the lifetime of that child feeling as though this longed-for dream was now killing her.'

I turned off the music, because the gated reverb on the drums seemed to give me the same kind of head-ache as the smell of hairdryers on moussed hair used to give me when I was very small, and because the purple light in the air – it was getting dark at three

49

o'clock every day, I found myself thinking – was as cold as the rest of the production on the album. The exultant choruses and the soaring guitars felt hysterical, as though they were brushing a painted ceiling without being able to break through. I pulled down the blinds, and lay down on my made bed, neither awake nor asleep, earplugs in, amazed by the silence and the darkness I'd found myself in. I hadn't found myself in this brackish darkness since the last time I'd gotten drunk: which had also been the first time. Why hadn't I come back to this solution sooner? If anything the drink had come too late; I'd been born, I realised, minus some final layer of skin that sealed others into their bodies and feelings and lives, my body forever ready to slip from that skin envelope, bundles of muscle and bone fixing to shunt and tumble with a loose wet thud to the floor, bundles spidered with more nerves than average, nerves that rang with a high-ratcheted volume of signal, most of it pain, no matter the occurrence – and so the salve and the sting of the first drink, my God, a relief craved for so long as to land upon me as obliteration.

I'd died. I'd fallen somewhere beyond sleep. It was class.

*

I first read Montaigne when I was nineteen, which is perhaps a bit too young. *To philosophise is to learn to die*: I was big into that. I hadn't figured out how to live but I'd heard that if you figured out how to die you'd learn how to live so I got into it. I was living in a student hall at the time, paid for by my family, and trying to get a scholarship so that they wouldn't have to pay for anything again this side of a PhD. The apartment was comfortable: a pod of electric light and heat. I was a malingerer in luxury. The colour scheme of these memories is an eyehurt of silver-white light and a cold, tundra lilac. These are drawn from the Luas that I got home every night at library closing time, and from the hard, standard-issue LEDs that lit my room. I wanted my apartment to be Montaigne's upstairs den, its dry warm smells of straw and upholstery, vellum pages, leather bindings. This light was so bony. So was the dark. At night I worked late with the help of Nescafé so strong that oilstain-coloured bubbles turned on the surface, and KitKat Chunkies from the vending machine. When I went to top up on the latter I'd go the long way back, via a stand of pine trees floored with rusted pine needles. I could have been anywhere when I stood there unwrapping my chocolate bar and hearing the wind move in the branches – a videogame Japan, on foggy nights; a scrap of campus in some US nowhere; a Pyrenean forest in the lee of a volcano. Once a heron zoomed silently past six inches from my nose. I envied the hard amber gleam of the eye that I saw in profile. I may as well not have been there at all, and I was haunted afterwards by a convulsionary sense of not having been or being all that I might have been or I was meant to become. A single wind-blasted uplit tree bare among the pines. I went back to my apartment and checked the *Guardian* for updates on Operation Cast Lead, jotting down Israeli casualties and

Palestinian casualties in the format of a football match. I did this every day. It was meant to make me grateful for where I was. It didn't work.

Nothing really worked. I'd been handcuffed to a greening corpse in the cell of a dungeon. I'd put the phone down on a girlfriend, in August of the previous year, while in Paris studying. I hadn't really been interested in anyone since. I remembered one night, before our breakup, dropping her home to her parents in deep Dublin 4, and getting what must have been the last Luas back from Sandyford Industrial Estate. The clock had said twenty minutes until the next one; the security guard breathing into the zipped-up collar of his anorak to keep his chin warm had confirmed this. I walked around the half-built towers hearing the sockets moan with the wind and the tarps flapping high up. The surname FARRELL was written in yellow font on a blue background. It was the same Farrell as the wealthy-smelling guy in my class who had gone off to check out Yale, Harvard and Stanford on a road trip with his father the summer before. By the time the Luas dinged and rolled into view I was freezing. The purple and silver lights all the way back towards my stop seemed if anything to make me colder. By the time I got in the door and put on the kettle for another Nescafé and got another KitKat Chunky out of the fridge, I was feeling like I hadn't come in from that cold at all, and was still walking around out there, up and down the winding paths that conjoined the dozens of unfinished and unfinishable developments stretching up around me, those anticipatory ruins of builders' rubble, bent piping, broken Wavin pipes, dark marl as rich as a split coal, rolls of rusted chicken wire. A long shard of the night felt as though it had lodged deep in me and wouldn't thaw. I opened a book to where I'd marked it with a folded strip of foil, then unwrapped the foil. Inside was a strip of acid tabs that I'd paid more for than I should have. Outwardly I was known for not drinking, but inwardly I wasn't a non-drinker: I was just trying to avoid drinking, because the first few times I'd done it I'd found an open door inside me that led to a zone of total, golden bliss so deep that I felt as if I mightn't come back from it. Acid was fine, though. Acid was that bit of Jonathan Swift's *Tale of a Tub* for me, the bit where he recommends the method of 'the modern learned', who should take fair correct copies bound in calf's skin and lettered at the back, of all modern bodies of arts and sciences, then boil them with opium or morphine in an alembic, until all that's left is a crusty black distillate that can be crushed into powder and huffed up the nose, where the little particles bloom as an infinite number of abstracts, summaries, compendiums, extracts, collections, medullas, excerpta quaedams, florilegia, all disposed into great order and reducible upon paper – so many fireworks rearing and blooming and drooping through the dark of the head in fine yellow scintillas and traceworks of warm red, green, silver, just this one big mell of euphoric light; all of knowledge, all at once, in an overdose of university. I sat for a long time in front of my collected Montaigne, frowning at the tabs and trying to think about what I liked. Mostly what I liked was the tea silence of the library late at night, padding around the bookshelves all but alone inside the place, or sitting up on the top floor of the Arts Block by the window looking down at the dead white shine of the old library, belltower, Front Arch apartments and Graduate Memorial Building, all of them neoclassical or something, all of their windows glowing with an amber warmth that made me think of some snug European heartland, insulated from history, from the present, from all the noise dinning in my head and which wouldn't go quiet no matter how much I tried to tire out my mind by pushing it down and along the tight corridors of the pages that I didn't so much read as live inside, since I found everything outside of them such an insufferable project. I don't think I found a solution for this until I found drugs and alcohol. Now that I don't drink alcohol or take drugs anymore, I'm back here again, and all I can do is wait this out.

Herodotus wrote, in his *Histories*, about a tribe who believed the soul lives in the head, which he found strange, because where he was from people believed it resided somewhere around the liver. When the chief of the tribe who believed that the soul was in the head captured his enemies, he would have their eyes, ears, nose and mouth sewn shut before they were decapitated, so their soul could not escape from the death of the body. I wonder about this at night when I put on my blindfold and screw in my earplugs. I wonder if I am really trying to keep the light and the noise out or if I am trying to keep something from leaking out of my skull – some fluxing black corrosion, one that eats holes in everything, one that makes even materiality scream.

*

By the time of the shit, I was wearing out. My girlfriend had gotten an offer for Cambridge, and then broken up with me. It made sense at the time. I couldn't afford to study in England and I'd a year to go before I graduated, anyway. She'd spoken of the end of our last summer together as an agony, but it'd been an idyll as far as I was concerned, wrapped up in the rug I'd bought her, in the cushioned dormer window of her family's big house in a small Irish coastal town, reading thick Victorian novels and watching the rain-fog creep back and forth over the treeline, while she waited to hear back on a job at a national newspaper, an editorial internship job, or that Master's in Oxford, while I spent the days we didn't see each other passing out on the couch at my parents' house, drunk on basic screwdrivers I'd fix myself and despondent from torrents of Ingmar Bergman films. She was rich. She'd be alright. She'd broken up with me over the phone, but she'd been sobbing. That made it hard to parse, as she'd have said. I'd write her long emails once a week. She'd reply to some of them. That was hard to parse, too.

Those days, when I drank, I'd be on Absolut, looking back and forth between book or screen and the winking bell-shaped litre-and-a-half bottles of what I thought of as liquid clarity. I wanted my head to ring with that same numbed clarity. *More heat than light*, a lecturer had said of one of my essays, or perhaps of all of them. Well, vodka made my head feel all light and no heat, pure white, a tundra nowhere, scalded into a clarity so painful that any other thought conceived outside of this state was pure retreat, a cowering away from the hard fact of being. Truth was a mixture of serenity and disgust: only the destroyed headspace of a vodka hangover got me to that place. The trouble was that, once there, it was too painful to write, and impossible to stop thinking, a kind of revving without forward motion – motor going ninety, wheels going nowhere. I reminded myself of those Buddhist monks I'd seen in a documentary once, the ones who'd drink only pinesap until they were painted sap-brown from within, mummified alive, their eyelids peeled away, the exposed eyes gone to dried acorns. This felt analogous, me there taking the world's chaos and contingency and destruction and channelling it directly at myself, as though this might cure my soul to that mummy texture, to that emptiness, getting me as close to death as possible while still alive.

I have the whole period edited down to as few memory frames as possible: how the cobblestones were mussel-shells in the swirling mud and rain; the toffee-coloured tiles of the Arts Block; the windowless, striplit tutorial rooms. I smoked rollies until the whorls of my fingertips turned dun, loving the cruise-speed feeling of booze and nicotine in my blood. I wrote a bad novel at the time as a kind of psychological Kleenex. I recall keeping the bottles in my room, to piss in, when the world was too blurry to move through. When my family called to visit we would meet somewhere else, off-campus.

During one such visit, at a pub, where I slugged down two Carlsbergs before lunch arrived, I remember my father biting the edge of his finger trying to hide how he felt about how I looked. I was ashen, having vomited into two different litter bins on my way to meet them. I was coming to the end of my final year, and it looked like I was going to be awarded another big academic prize. But even if my family had been able to afford them, I'd missed all of the deadlines for the kind of university I should have been applying for. The word burnout, with its sharp yellow smell, the noise of a lightbulb filament about to go, had started to hover in the air.

I talked vaguely and too quickly about moving to Prague after graduating.

'To do what?'

'I think I want to do nothing for a while.' My voice had a plea in it.

'You can't do nothing. We all have to earn a living. That's how the world works.'

I order another pint when the waitress swoops in for my empty glass.

'It's one o'clock, Tim.'

'I got up early. What are you drinking?'

Da indicated his forlorn, failed tea, his acrid coffee. 'Not impressed so far,' he says. 'Perhaps some water!' The hope is bright in his voice. 'They can't mess up water, can they?'

'Spirochetes,' I say.

*

When my final grades came in, they were very high. I did end up going to Prague, but not to live. I went with my father just before college finished. It was his pat on the back for getting through the years of academic toil.

Prague by night through the aeroplane window was an orange spill, the same shape as protozoa.

'This is how we look to God,' I slurred to Da, who frowned.

'Never heard of him.'

'Do you want another sandwich?' I asked him. 'I can arrange that. Anything you want. It's all on me. Pringles, Kinder Bueno, a fucking choc-ice, if it's on the flight trolley it'll be in your gob soon as kiss hands, my friend!'

Benzos only kind of work on me, I was discovering. My pulse was still a flutter. My lungs seemed to fill only half the way up.

Down, now, through the fiery wool of the clouds. My gut lurches.

'The spirochetes in Prague are huge,' says my da. 'I learned that from Kafka. Probably.'

One night on that trip, coming in from a bar, while Da's sleeping, I bucket up dark red sick and think it's blood. But then I see black threads – my stomach lining – meaning the red isn't blood but sugar. My liver is a dark bruise, mid-torso. I lean my head on the cold rim of the bowl. My hangover has already begun: a fruit-rotty heat in the skull. I have a licked-battery taste on my tongue.

In Prague the TV blarted an endless static phrase at us from its white screen. Flicking the channels we found a quieter channel across which jerked thin bands of white.

'You can make out a footballer through the snow,' said my da.

'Cut in slices, though.'

'Do you want to go back to the salt mines again, is it?'

I pictured the salt miners in the blue mica-glinting caverns of Wieliczka, pictured their hands' seams whitening with ingrained salt, pictured the salt coating their fingers until they were blue with ingrained salt.

'Nah, man,' I said. 'They felt very literal.' My tongue is fat with benzos and my thoughts are treacly.

Da frowns and paws the air. 'Me book.' I hand it to him. We read. Well, he read. I took the words in, but thoughtlessly, as if they were so many bytes in data transfer. I hear my own brain make the light gritting noise of a hard drive. Soon I wasn't even reading, instead I was just letting my eyes skate over the white gaps between words, so many iced-under pools, elongated, thin-surfaced, the kind you fall down through easily; there was the sound of my father's breath slowing as he dozed, and my worry about when he would die.

*

When I got back from Prague – benzos and wine all night; magmatic black shits and sweaty thunderous migraines all morning; sunglassed, pasty-faced sightseeing all afternoons: curative, ultimately, of any desire to return to Prague, still less live there – my writer friend, the one from Freshers' Week, had become an editor. I remember us sitting on the bed of my last room in college. The broken ring of people sitting in the circle on my floor were talking. One of them was twanging at my unplugged guitar – some kind of funk-adjacent Hendrix-style riffing that didn't sound at all bad.

'Tell me about the guitar,' he'd said, in the unctuous voice of a therapist, as if he had begun to find all of this desperation disturbing. That made the feeling of a cat arching its back ripple through my upper body. I shrugged and said I got a lot out of distracting myself that was nothing to do with my head or my words or whatever. He told me that this was good, a positive, because I read too many books.

'You read the way you drink and do drugs,' he said. 'It's an addiction. You're trying to do something to yourself with them that they can't do.'

I didn't say anything. I just looked at the pile of books I had yet to read teetering in their stacks on the coffee table. I was forever bumping my hip against them.

'It's almost as if,' the young editor said, 'you're one of those kids who are born into a bilingual family; can't say anything until they're seven or eight, and then they're word-perfect in both languages. You're the same, because you have put so much in your head – too much, maybe.'

What he said hurt and that meant it must be true. Hurt was the only measure of truth I had left. Outside, cars sluiced down Pearse Street under the dirty wet lights – red, green, blue. The scraping noise was almost peaceful. It rasped my thoughts in half. I couldn't feel them anymore. I don't remember what I was on: probably only drink; I remember I was pretty broke that weekend, didn't eat. I bobbed my head, lips pursed, said, 'Yeah, maybe, that's a good point,' the way I did whenever someone countered an argument against one of my points in a tutorial and I found it to be total arse gravy.

The other people in my room, I don't think they could hear this review of my personality. I felt glad of that at the time. But maybe if they had, and maybe if someone had scoffed at what he'd said, or suggested, 'That's a bit weird,' or 'That's a bit much,' or 'That's a bit condescending,' maybe then the personality-review wouldn't still be echoing in my head, making my blood seethe with anger, seethe and fizz like something cooking in a burnt-black spoon.

*

That college friend forwarded my manuscript to an editor at a small but prestigious publishing house. The editor did not enjoy the novel. He tattooed the margins of the document with snide remarks of the kind that we all write, I suppose, when a piece of work really is that bad. But he offered, in his email, to meet me – I suspect as a favour to my friend, who was in turn doing me a favour – though he added to the invite, *I am sure you would prefer to throw acid on me.* This wasn't true: I was too crushed to feel angry or, at least, I didn't feel angry until our meeting, in the upstairs café in the branch of Tower Records that used to be on Wicklow Street. I had no clean clothes other than a white shirt, so I ended up accidentally overdressed for the occasion, with the black overcoat I owned over the top, because I didn't have any jumpers left whose sleeves weren't holed by fallen bits of lit cigarettes or joints. It was the first time I'd met an editor. He was nice, shy, diffident, but in my arrogance I found this dweebish, almost pitiable.

It should be noted here that I had been drinking most of the morning. The editor told me that the important thing to remember about writing is that I was insignificant not just in the grand but also in any kind of scheme of things, and that this understanding ought to be a starting point for my future work. He told me not to rush into publication, because a lot of people he knew who took writing seriously weren't getting books out until they were around his age, which I assumed to be somewhere in his early forties. I asked him what I should be doing at this age, in that case, and he told me to go away and find something to write about, then see what my options might be, because what I'd written was the kind of novel people write when they think they have a worse substance abuse problem than they in fact do.

I have never really stopped feeling what I felt in that moment – as though a small, pointed depth-charge had exploded against the middle of my chest. *I'll show you,* I thought. *I'll show you how bad it is.* This is a dangerous feeling still to hold in my body. Anger feels to me the way cocaine used to: something happens to infuriate me, I feel the sharp bitter dart of the snort going up my sinus, and then there's eight seconds of a lapse before a rippling wave of heat crosses diagonally from my left shoulder to the bottom-most rib on the right side of my chest. My eye kicks thinking of the remembered anger. Under the heat there comes an upward rush of a dark, cold and extremely self-serious fury, from the pit of my stomach to the roof of my mouth. It's the most nihilistic sensation I have in my body still, even after so many years away from drugs and alcohol. *You don't know a thing,* the sensation says, *but I'll show you, you posh cunt.*

I wish I knew where the anger comes from. It was there before I knew what class was. It was there before the frustration of my writing being rejected took on such towering proportions inside me. I think it must have been there when I was a baby, or at least a small child, and that I must have rediscovered the feeling of rage through the burning sensation of alcohol. I can't seem to get any further back than this memory, though, which is of me, aged about four, one Saturday evening of whipping wind, hard rain and black sky beyond the sitting-room windows. A fire is roaring in the grate. It's the exact same shape as the Disney castle at the start of all the films. I'm thinking about this and only this, because I have a fever, and I'm sweating, and my throat is so tight with heat that I can't call for anybody. My stomach has been hurting all day. I keep wanting to vomit but anytime I've been to the toilet all that comes out is a searing, watery spatter of shit. All I've been able to do is lie there face down on the carpet with my picture book about the kings and queens of England, reading about how they died. I read that story about Henry I and the poisoned eels, and my insides eel around, too, at once cooked and hot and still alive and writhing around under my skin. I want them to swim out of me and leave me empty. This does not happen. I'm stuck inside the shrinking form of my own body, which is tightening and sweating. If this goes on too much longer, something is going to buckle or die, I'm sure of it. I look down into the carpet. The red of it is pocked all over with white diamonds that have little black pupil-dots at their centres. I become convinced that the entire world is nothing more than strings of this sensation, these varying gradations of hard and soft. This is all the world is now: textures moving in the dark. At the bottom there isn't even nothing; it's the same as the well I'd seen Gaston fall into at the end of *Beauty and the Beast*, a hole that's nothing only the fall. There is only the falling, and eventually I'll stop being aware of it, and that'll be it: no more me. Suddenly I feel warm arms swooping me up. They're my father's. He's carrying me up the stairs. My sister is also ill and I'm being carried towards her. She's sitting up in my parents' bed, a big snowy drift of duvet high around her, a chip on her fork. My mother is a still presence in the background and the air is tinselled with the certainty that she is smiling. I should feel peace. But I feel nothing but the sensation of the words *Where were you when I needed you?* being screamed from the reddest, rawest depths of my body. It is the feeling of not having been listened to – a fact bitterly resented, even though I hadn't, in fact, been able to make any sound at all. There had only been the crackle and sputter of the fire in the grate, the whistling noise of the wind in the chimney, the whipping rain.

*

One Sunday in 2011, still staggering from the previous night's pills, body still quaking around the bass of a Benga gig that had climaxed with noises like tarmac roads melting and warping and rising against each other in waves of rich hot black, I went out of the campus onto Nassau Street, crossed the road to the Spar, and saw a strangely familiar figure bent over, his hands crossed at the small of

64

his back, squinting at a rotating display of postcards – pub doors of Ireland, Great Irish Writers, pints of Guinness. I thought the familiar-looking man was Paul Muldoon, and I wanted to stop, but I wasn't sure it was him, and I also wasn't sure how long my guts were going to hold steady. I gathered up the three bottles and paid with my Laser card, quickly, as if that made a difference, because I didn't know if there was enough money in my account. Monday would be a long and hungry day, but someone had left a few cans in my fridge, and I could always just have sleep for dinner. Paul Muldoon was wearing a big spotted tie and a black shirt. It was definitely him. The ellipsis on the terminal blipped and erased itself, blipped and erased itself, formed a circle that turned against digital nothing, and I kept my fingers crossed behind my back until the receipt chugged out and I could go. I'm not sure how seriously I'd considered asking Paul Muldoon to spot me money should my card be declined, but there was no need for that now. The relief expanded in my chest. I went up to him.

'Are you Paul Muldoon?' I said.

'Oh!' He stood up with a start, his hand out, his face blank and cheerful. 'Yes. Paul Muldoon. Nice to meet you.'

I shook his hand and told him I'd enjoyed his Baudelaire translation in *Maggot*.

'Oh!' he said again. He looked chuffed. He gave a little quirk of the head and smiled with one side of his mouth. I thought this was gracious of him. I'd seen myself on my way here, smelled myself, too, breathed in that greenish tang of late vegetable decay rising out of my pores. Fair play to him, I thought.

'What has you back?' I said.

'I'm doing a reading over there.' He pointed, squinting. 'Conference Centre.'

'The one that looks like a can. Yes.'

'Yes.' His squint deepened behind his glasses. Clouds shifted. A brassy strike of light darkened the lenses. 'We're commemorating 9/11.'

'Right.' A sudden kick of pain went off in the upper corner of my head, a bass-drum pedal turned around so the hard heel of plastic could really ding it. 'That's cool.'

'Yes. They've all been very nice.'

'Well, have fun, anyway,' I said. Now my eyes were narrowed. There were headrush stars teeming everywhere. 'I'll chat to you.'

He put his hand out again and said, 'Well, it's been a pleasure.'

'Yeah, same.' I shook. The grip was cool and soft. I tried to remember this. I was a punchline. I'd wanted a laying-on of hands from greatness for going on five years now, and now it had finally come, early on a Sunday morning, in circumstances that could not be turned into anything, at a time when the only thing I was capable of was falling through the door of my apartment and drinking on the bed until the Spire in the distance turned to a spike of caught morning light.

'Good luck with it all, anyway,' I said, and he gave me a little salute and turned back to the postcards, stooping, squinting. I crossed the road. I went home. I got drunk. I went to sleep. In the years that followed, I kept waiting for those postcards to turn up in one of Paul Muldoon's poems.

*

66

I worked hard all week, all day, into the night, then got drunk to make myself pass out. This was about a year and a half into the troika – the IMF, the European Central Bank and the European Commission – stepping in to help the crypto-Thatcherites in government implement the kind of austerity measures that not even they had the guts to apply to their fullest extent. Dublin felt as though it was freezing over. Winter lasted about eighteen months that year.

Friday nights I would go to a Catholic-run soup kitchen – it was the only one I knew of – and politely nod and grimace my way through the bad opinions about abortion to bring sandwiches and coffees and chocolate bars to homeless people. There were more every week. The stories became sadder every week, too. I remember one guy gashing his neck with a can and sobbing. 'He's alright,' his friend said, patting him on the shoulder. 'It's not youse he's angry at.' I gave the friend food to pass on to the can-guy. I dropped in an extra Penguin bar. That had been sad, but you got used to the rest fairly quickly. Anytime you came across a guy injecting heroin into the one good vein left in his dick you wouldn't even say 'C'mon, man' anymore: you'd just ask him how many sugars he wanted in his coffee, and he wouldn't stop injecting, he'd just say 'Six' or 'Seven' or whatever. Probably we'd have dropped in more, but there weren't many left, and it was still early in the night.

Another guy I met that evening had been a computer programmer for a bank until about three weeks before. He couldn't believe he was sitting on the Ha'penny Bridge begging for change, either. He just looked stunned. You could hear the shyness in his voice. An older man who stuck around Temple Bar would tell us about friends of his who'd died in recent weeks, making a litany of their names. We didn't know who they were, but he didn't have anybody else to tell.

I'd had a lot of friends in college. You could take me anywhere and I'd find someone to get on with. I used to feel myself glittering all over in company. It took me out of myself, made me someone else to other people. When they went away, I'd feel that attention turn over in my head, become something darker, inverted. The wall of my skull seethed all over with shinily insectile eyes. So, nothing ever went so deep with people, even though I always had people saying 'Hello' or stopping to chat or whatever while I asked them about how things were. I didn't feel any bond or blurring of our lives' outlines with each other. It was all contiguous, billiard balls bumping against each other, settling with a deep cluck curve to curve. Apparent closeness is probably the most distancing thing of all, and I did it because I thought and still think that love's an ugly, clawed, scraping thing, and I felt sure that getting close to me would unleash that in me.

What was worse was that so many of these friends had gone to London that even the vintage soul night we would go to had relocated to some equivalent bar over there. Others had their evenings gobbled up by unpaid internships, or had gotten jobs in the civil service and were caught up in endless exams, or were doing MAs, or had gone back to live with their parents. My privately educated friends trampolined beyond Trinity's walls and on to what one of my lecturers had called 'the royal road': Oxford, Harvard, Princeton. One lecturer had mentioned the École Normale Supérieure in Paris to me, but I'd felt a jag of fear at the thought, thinking that maybe I really would end up doing something fatally stupid if let loose in Paris. The weight in my body had been too immense to even contemplate filling in the forms. Every rung in my social ladder appeared to be giving way beneath me. But I had to hold on there for a while yet. I had no other option.

I stuck together a tentative doctoral proposal: Dante, melancholia, Joyce. I read about the history of depression, the melancholy raptures that lifted Socrates out of his body, a preparation for death. I read Avicenna's theory on the burnt bile, burnt phlegm and burnt blood that created a dark powder symptomatic of visionary overheating. The all-night reading room and the cool purple glow of the vending machines, the shadows and silences of the library, corridor after corridor, the unfoldings of a hotel of the dead in some kind of dream, the dives into despair was a truer, purer success – uninsulated, the real thing.

The scholarship I'd won in my second undergraduate year meant that I didn't have to pay rent on my apartment. I had an internship at a mental health charity that occasionally involved payment. I'd won a small academic prize. I had four hours a week doing data-entry at a self-publishing business. That, I decided, would have to be enough until year two of the doctorate, when I might have the chance to teach.

One afternoon I went to the cinema with a friend who'd taken a sabbatical year to run a student society.

En route, he told me that he'd been accepted into Stanford's Ancient Philosophy programme pending his fourth-year results. His news made the evening blur and shimmer. Sun flared orange over the redbricks and glass. I looked at the Coca-Cola I'd gotten at a takeaway and saw the fluming browns and candy-striped straws morph and move. I wanted to be lost in that space. I wanted to tip a naggin into the litre cup.

'Huh,' I said, and then, 'Congratulations.'

'If we don't get nuked, of course,' my friend said, with a chuckle that I decided sounded guilty. 'There was something on the news about Kim Jong-un running nuclear tests, about the US making bellicose noises.'

I don't remember what film we saw. I was watching the walls judder apart, a vast pair of jaws, the screen tearing and the world's entire unbought glut of supermarket cabbages, rainbow shoals of DVDs, sweet wrappers, the whole bright trash heap spilling into the gap and washing me away with it. Walking home in silence, I remembered feeling sure – the way I had done when I was a small child – that the mortar between the bricks of the buildings was about to leap out at me, a tinkling rubble of tongues while everything cascaded down over me; tongues of mortar, tongues of rotting plaster, tongueshapes of bricks that sheeted down from demolition, noise like shattering glass, for ever and ever amen, horizon boiling with dust, swallowing my breath, my tongue.

It must have been around this time that I found where the campus maintenance lads kept the key to the roof, and that night, after the cinema I decided to drink my last bottle of the day while perched on the ledge, looking down on the din and the mess. I'd gotten good at finding ways to access these roofs.

One of my favourites to sit on at night was atop the Geology building. Heights didn't scare me when I was drunk: just the rest of the time. I'd always been terrified of heights, even if I wasn't up in a high place myself. As a child, during trips to Dublin, I would cower in the back seat or become dizzy while walking the streets, for fear of the buildings toppling over us. I have always been subject to these terrors, these visions. When I was perhaps six or seven, I saw the banshee from *Darby O'Gill and the Little People* looming out from the dark of my sister's room across the hall. I became so hysterical that my sister also began to see the fucking thing looming out at her.

These nightmarish dreams felt retrospectively prophetic, a foretelling of the world I'd die in. My head was busy with images of the end. Opening a Styrofoam takeaway tray, I'd see white pellets choking the fish. When I washed my hair I could smell the oceans turning to acid. Looking up at a clean winter's sky, one single jet contrail was enough to make me imagine the pollutants turning the ice in the clouds into slush. I'd read somewhere that people's diets contain so much mercury that the last thing to disappear of our civilisation would be the silver lakelets where public toilets once had been, before the churn of geology worked everything under again.

Even reading provided no escape. I could no longer tolerate bookshops, especially not those with a big second-hand collection. The packed shelves turned to the back streets where I did my lone drinking, stinking of disinfectant and of whatever rottenness the disinfectant was meant to hide. The sour tang of their pages made me feel rain on my skin, and the lines of print became streets in some mournful mid-European city, with old games machines that weren't vintage, just old, and nights that felt like a black rain mac slick with rain, a city of literature that morphed periodically into a Borgesian landscape, where the sheer quantity of words and pages and thoughts seemed to argue that every possible permutation of human pain had already been written out and published and forgotten, with nothing new to add, with all of me accounted for in advance.

Now, half pissed, a little stoned, I looked blearily down at the place where the skin of the road had been peeled back, baring a black soup of mud and dirt and gravel and pale, straggling tree-roots, none of it holding any bones, or ruins: just a swirl of sand and gypsum and tarmac gone inky in the leakage underground, an eddy in an oil-spill pool. They were at that messy stage of the project where the idea of a smooth, new road looks further away than if they hadn't even bothered to start work. I was looking down on an anticipatory ruin, looking down on the way things would look when they had been worn away completely.

I didn't hear the door to the roof open behind me, didn't notice the new presence up there with me until the shadow fell across my body.

'Ah, fuck,' I said, and I instinctively jumped back, slipped, steadied myself against a chimneybreast.

'You're alright, you're alright,' the man said.

I knew him; let's call him Barry. He was one of the security guards, one of the sound ones. He had a way of sighing and shaking his head when he turned up at house parties that made him seem like he hated what he was doing as much as we did. Once my ex-girlfriend and my flatmate and I had chucked pots of water down on top of some noisy student-union types who were smoking and talking bollocks outside of our window. Barry had come up afterwards, grinning, inviting us to play dumb, saying, 'You wouldn't know anything about a bunch of lads getting soaked under this window, would you?' But he wasn't grinning this evening. He looked worried.

'What's the craic,' I said, and dropped the joint down the neck of my wine-bottle. I heard the sizzle. I saw his eyes move to the bottle and back to my face. 'It's just a smoke,' I said. 'Standard issue.'

He shook his head. 'I can recognise the smell.'

'Yeah?'

'You'll remember this is a university.'

'Oh. Yeah.'

Barry squinted around the rooftop, breathing out. 'Look, you know you're not meant to be up here, but you weren't about to do anything stupid, were you?'

'Like what?'

He gave a click of the tongue and a bob of the head. 'Well, I don't know,' he said. 'Like throw yourself off or something?'

'Jesus.'

'I'm not hearing "No",' he said, then he looked back down the way he'd come. He jerked his head, said, 'Look, come on down from up here, will you? And we can have a chat about it, alright? There's nothing going to happen. It's OK.'

I was too embarrassed to protest, and so I just followed him down the stairs. He walked me across Front Square to the security booth under the arch.

'What happened to you, anyway?'

'Breakup,' I said.

'Shite.' Barry sucked his teeth, then pushed open the glass door to the booth under Front Arch. The smell inside was of instant coffee and Johnny Blue. He lifted the partition in the desk and said, 'On you go. Grab yourself a chair there.'

I did as he said while he unlocked and pulled out a drawer, which clinked with all the bottles inside – Jameson, Huzzar, Green Spot, the whole lot.

'You can guess where we pick these up from.'

'Yeah.'

He wavered his fingers above the collection, slid out the Green Spot. 'There should be at least one clean cup in the back kitchen there.'

'You don't want one?'

'Working, aren't I,' he said. He plonked a packet of cigarettes down on the table in front of me. 'You OK here for a bit?'

'I'm fine,' I said, sliding one from the packet and putting it behind my ear. 'I could honestly go back home.'

Barry scratched his ear. 'See, here's the thing. If we think someone's going to hurt themselves or someone else, well, it's either we call the guards or we just sort of . . . I guess, wait? For either the doctor to come on call or wait for them to look a bit better.'

Hearing that, I felt a cold, skin-rippling rush of fear. My flatmate's father had killed himself at Christmas. In the silence around the news, I'd asked my flatmate how the holidays had been. He laughed and said, 'Other than that, Mrs Lincoln, how was the play?' When my face fell and I started to gabble out apologies, he was the one who ended up consoling me with a pat on the shoulder and saying not to worry, that making fun of it was the best way through. After he'd moved home, the news hung around his room, same as the smell when the drain of our kitchen sink got blocked, a treacle-murk rot-stink tacking itself to everything.

'I'm alright,' I managed to say to Barry. 'Honestly.'

Barry's mouth was a concerned line. 'No offence or anything, but, well. You wouldn't be looking a hundred per cent to me.' He handed me the cup. 'I do paintballing. Lads go into shock and all. And you gave yourself a fright there, tottering on the roof I think. So, a dram is usually the fastest thing, to be honest.'

I swirled the cup and golloped it down like it was nothing, only juice.

'Are mental health services really that bad?' I said. 'That you're giving whiskey to people you think might be a suicide risk?'

He spread his hands and said, 'Twelve on the campus this year. I'll fucking try anything at this point.' His voice was glib. His eyes were not.

'Twelve?'

He counted, starting with the little finger of his left hand. 'Three overdoses, two hangings from belts around doorhandles, and the rest did the wrist thing with a bucket of warm water – you'll have noticed youse have no baths in your gaffs. This is why.' He tutted. 'But sure, fuckit. Nature finds a fucking way, doesn't it.'

'You must get used to it, no?'

'Not at all.'

He took the other chair and looked at the squares of CCTV footage jumping from one to the other. An extra screen flickered beside the one rigged up to all the cameras. It appeared to show a video game that had been paused. The frozen image on the screen reminded me of light streaming through the birches my father and I had planted years before, back home. I remembered everything about planting them, the soft grunt of the earth giving way under the shovel, the coppery taper of their roots, as delicate as the inside of fuses, the foggy light through them when we'd finished. They'd been burned ages ago. Da had gotten sick of sweeping up the yellow seedpods that flurried over the tarmac; plus, they'd gotten sick, too, with a blighting tree disease, some of them; gravesmelling black scutter leaking out of their cores when we'd split their trunks with the axe, not even good for firewood in the end.

The first sip hit and I felt better instantly – numb, tingly, giddy with relief, as though the world were solid, but soft, made of clouds, or the pillowy whiteness in that Softmints ad from the nineties: a warm cloudiness that could support my weight, but wouldn't hurt if I fell down. It was, I thought as I took my second sip, always so easy to get to that place.

*

76

I was actually quite old – seventeen – before I'd first sensed the possibility of that pillowy softness. We'd been reading about alcoholism in religion class. One testimony from a recovering alcoholic was printed against a blue sky. The point of the thing was to put us off drink, but all that happened was I felt enticed – how could I not, in one way, reading the words *The first time I drank, I felt safe* printed against pale blue air and Super Mario clouds, through which God himself might reach down and hand a sticky bottle of something to me? I'd grown up knowing that a relative had what was referred to as a 'drink problem'. He was the one I looked most like, acted most like, talked most like, moved my hands the most like, laughed the most like, got giddy the most like. Once, when I'd been reading a book as a small child, I'd asked him what the word 'jubilant' meant. He'd told me the answer in a deep voice tarry with cigarettes. It sounded warm to me, *jubilant, jubilant*, inseparable from the sound of his voice, the cosy party smell of his clothes. I'd smelled his body, that warmish fug of cigarettes and sour beer, and clocked the smile that was always about to wobble off his face. It didn't seem the worst way to be, but my mother used to clutch her temples and say, 'Oh, Lord', and then his name, as though that were the start of a prayer, whenever a reminder of him came up in conversation, as though measuring the love she had for him by the pain she allowed him to cause her.

From the classroom where I read the blue-sky words of that man who felt 'safe' when he first drank alcohol, I could see the cathedral where I'd been baptised,

St Mary's, the spire looking cleansed by the harsh cool of the autumn sun. Inside was a wax statue of a saint lying in her death throes, with a tin chalice of her ostensible blood held between her hands. An image of that chalice hovered in my head, and the chalice contained alcohol. That was what peace looked like.

It was a half-day at school. I went straight to the drinks cabinet. It wasn't me opening the front door, going into the sitting room, kneeling at the cabinet, doing a quick assessment, then leathering into it with the free Bailey's glass that my mother had gotten in a two-for-one offer a couple of weeks before. That safety feeling hit almost immediately, a warm amniotic thrum. The outline of my body seemed to waver then resolve into golden undulations. My heartbeat was no longer an anxious kick in the chest, but slowed to fantails of candy-coloured fireworks that arced through a midnight void. I felt great, in other words. There may have been an itch of fear under the soft heat of my second Southern Comfort sour, mixed from ingredients left over from Pancake Tuesday, according to instructions on the back of the label. But the only thing that really frightened me at all in that moment was how well the stuff worked.

When my father came home to find me groaning and already hungover under the covers of my bed, a part of me wanted him to realise what he was seeing and smelling, wanted him to zero in on the sticky Southern Comfort tang breathing from my pores. I wanted him to rip back the veil.

'I'll leave you to it, so,' he said, after listening to me groan for a while. He shut the door. I woke up later, showered, went downstairs, feeling clean and rinsed and scot-free. I think we watched *Michael Clayton* together, afterwards.

It wasn't the last time he'd catch me, and then continue as though nothing had happened. I can't really remember how these encounters played themselves out. My memory holds only the record of my father's face, of each gradation in his expression from concern to exhaustion with the very person he had been concerned about.

A few months before my evening with the college security guy, when I was leaving my flat for the summer, my father drove me home in cold silence, until around as far as Goff's on the N7. At last, he said, 'Do you think you have a drink problem?' I will never forget the sensation: a mixture of extreme heat and extreme cold flaring up along my body, and my skin rippling as if in the updraught of a plane lifting off directly in front of me. I was neither dead nor alive.

'What?' I said, trying to add a sceptical uplift to my voice.

Dad tutted, sighed, said, 'It's Mick saying it,' mentioning the name of an old friend. 'He saw you at a party with the lads back home. Out one weekend. Said youse drank the way old men do, downing a pint and a shot every go. Going wild. But, well.' He paused, fixed his gaze through the windscreen. 'His sons have had enough struggles.'

My innards jounced up and down, but still I could speak. 'He'd know,' I said. My father said nothing. 'His sons had troubles, didn't they?' I said.

Dad kept his eyes on the road. The sky was the pink and unforgiving silver of a Superser heater coming on. When I'd been a teenager, when I'd fuck up – get less than a ninety on a test, come home with the smell of Marlboro Red on me, mix up the times for a debating trip or an after-school practice and leave myself without a lift – Dad and my ma would sit me down and excoriate me for hours, telling me everything that was bad about me, linking minor flaws to deep, inherited similarities between me and their problematic siblings. I'd try to interrupt, to tell them that I was in immense pain, but every time I would be told that I was trying to get myself off the hook.

But now my father had hit on what was really going wrong inside me, and now I wanted him to finish the job of peeling all of my flaws into visibility. I wanted the tarp to be pulled off everything I'd gotten up to. I wanted the sputter of fat, the cleansing, excoriating punishment of it.

My father flipped the indicator, tutted and shifted lanes.

'But you know Mick,' he said. 'He might just be being spiteful, either. He is always trying to pull me down. Making it sound like his problems are the ones that I have.'

I looked at my father. He kept looking at the road.

'Don't mind him,' he said. 'Forget about it.'

We pulled into Castledermot. We got chips and ate them sitting on the bonnet of the car, same as the one evening when I'd been eight or so we'd had Creme Eggs while the town lights yellowed the gaps between the cobblestones. As we ate, I remember each hot bite of the chips stinging to the cores of my teeth. I was glad of the carb weight in my belly. That morning I'd woken bloody knuckled in the empty yard of a primary school and walked down to the rippling waters at Grand Canal Dock, trying to decide whether I should walk all the way to St Pat's, check myself in. As part of my work with the mental health charity I had been on a panel interviewing psychiatrists for a new teen unit; now I wondered if mentioning this credential at the door of the psychiatric hospital would get me into a ward. I wanted to be hugged around the head with deep, white blankets and told that I was alright, hugged and told until the permaclutch of my muscles relaxed. Eventually, instead of St Pat's, I had gone into the Spar, gotten a wedge roll, a bottle of Jack Daniel's and a load of blackcurrant, then spent the morning drinking and swaying in front of the pristine unread books I'd bought for my PhD.

My father ate quickly, with a hunted blankness in his eyes. I looked at him and even though he and everyone else was letting me slide out of view I found it impossible to hate him. That look on his face – slow blinks, eyes milky with childneed – was the look he got eating in front of the TV at home, and it was so easy to see him decades before watching a Western or the sports or the football and wishing he was one of the cowboys, one of the boxers, one of the footballers, one of the actors playing one of the cowboys. Unspecified financial stress had come down on our house: nobody would say what; the papers filled in the blanks. There were times I saw his forehead take on the shiny pallor of a rasher being fried, other times when a blue hashtag of pressurised veins appeared at his temple. I knew he wouldn't be able to carry me if I needed him. I had to carry him. I had to keep this back.

The cars were trailing past my da and me. The air was tart with woodsmoke. A cold wind raked my sore knuckles.

'We'll go on home, will we?' Da said, and I got back into the car with him.

*

I felt myself slump down along the little pleather bench in the security booth, watching a cloud of moths and flittering cigarette ash turn in the square of light by the door, above where Barry was smoking. The same grey shreds were turning above his head now, joining with the drizzle under the lights, making the funnel shapes that mackerel form up into when threatened. He watched them, looking peaceful, and then his radio yawked and he shook his head, tutted, flicked his cigarette and turned to me, saying, 'I won't be ten minutes.'

'Not a problem,' I said, and toasted him with the cup. Then, when he was out of sight, I slugged off the rest, slipped out of the booth with the bottle of Green Spot inside my coat and went out onto College Green, bending my steps around the corner, heading east, making for the sea.

If what comes next seems like a big jump, then it's because it's a logistical issue. It doesn't seem like one in my memory. I go from the weekend I told my family I was dropping out of my doctoral programme, which returns as an image of me sitting on the floor of the room where my sister had her piano. My sister, mother, and father are all standing over me. Shouting is happening. I don't know whose: it could even be mine, although it can't be that loud if it's me doing the shouting, because I'm holding my forehead pinned against my knees, my arms shielding the top of my head, my parents stand in the doorway, saying nothing. I don't remember words, only noise, and I can't remember from where: only a steam heat raining down, both inside and outside my skull, but with a seam of clarity tapering in a serif through the middle of all the howling, a wordless sureness that I was right to be getting out of there. What else comes between that moment and the time on the plane is not a blur: it's a nothing. I know based on receipts and emails that in between is a summer that involved meeting my then-girlfriend and an autumn doing a teacher training course in Barcelona. Memories come of those times. But when I hold the picture in my head of my parents and my sister standing over me, the four of us caught in the lee of that awful serrated barracking, there's a jump, a wobble: the picture skips, there's a gap, and next thing I'm walking along the travelator in Frankfurt Airport, passing decorative brass plates stuck to the walls that throw back my reflection chopped into a crosshatching of scratchy lines, thinking of that Borges line about how there's always a mirror that's seen me for the last time. Then I'm snapping awake, seeing my girlfriend's silhouette through the canvas screen separating baggage collection from Arrivals at the airport in Brasília. Then it's all the bad stuff that happened there.

When I try to access the images conjoining this period to that, all I hear is a clunk in my head: *FILE NOT FOUND*. It took me a long time to find a way to explain this. I'd always thought it was so obvious that people had vast tracts of their own lives that just aren't there. And I thought, too, that when other people tried to access their stuff under the black weightiness that their mental surfaces tossed, rose, raged, made them flail or grow silent, made them lie foetal and tearful on any given floor, forehead to the metal, forehead to the tile, forehead to the lino, forehead to the scratchy carpet, desperate to cool away the threat of those memories and their return.

Maybe you don't find yourself on those floors. Hard luck if you don't. I used to love blackouts. Under anaesthetic for operations, you may have had a taste of that total nothing feeling: a skip, a gap, as though you've ceased. The trouble kicks in when you come back – that hard punch of the breath's renewed insuck waking up, out of nothing, into being, and the raw wrenching pain of that, a branch pulling itself loose from the meat of your chest, as the horror of resumption comes in on you.

I wish there were words that gave me back that velvet nothing feeling, gave me back to that nowhere place. Let me try. I want to say *obsidian lake.* I want to imagine the splash of those waters, how they throw up drops that spatter and fizz and corrode a million hissing tiny holes in the memories around them. I can't remember the blackouts, I can't remember the things around the blackouts, I'd love to be able to forget like that again, I'd love to step into the cold of that lake – that cold so total it amputates first my toes and then my feet and then my shins and then my upper legs and then everything up to the waist and then everything above that too. The air smells of milled stone, the marl and gravel and silt you find when you pry a cobblestone from its socket.

But it's not just the memory holes that defeat the straight line, the three-act structure, the sense that this is a memoir. It's the fact that I don't want to remember. Forgetting was bliss beyond name to me. Those slow, years-long deletions, by needle, by bottle, by baggie: they were an aesthetic project to me. Putting things back together? Putting things in order? What about the void, what about unwriting, what about forgetting? Forget inscription: what about *ex*scription, scratching the words out onto your ear so they're not in me anymore? What about *expression* in the sense of cutting an 'X' into the surface of a fat sore on a knee, then pushing out all the pus until it breathes itself empty?

Forgetting's the real stuff – the transience, the dissolution, the things not being there even while your head's processing the sensory matter in such a way that you feel momentarily convinced that there's a real world around you. The black pool is the truth: that fluxing, consuming, liverblack nothing, eating it all away, and here we are, sinking, up to our knees in it.

*

After dropping out of my doctoral programme, I met a woman whose visa was about to run out and so she would be returning to her home city, Brasília. I went with her because there was fuck-all keeping me in Ireland that wasn't also killing me. She rented an apartment from a lawyer friend of hers, in one of the new suburbs on the outskirts of the city. The whole district was a building site: shiny high rises abutting on a nothingscape of rolling hills, specked with the white dice of luxury villas. We didn't live in one of those. We lived on the fifteenth floor of a building that wasn't finished, and was next door to the clatteringly loud site of another building that wasn't finished. The noise woke us daily, punctually at 5 a.m. I couldn't keep up in Portuguese when we were with her friends. Everything I managed to say when I wasn't wasted seemed to drop onto the table in silence, a cat bringing an unwanted chunk of mouse. She left me for someone else. This felt fair: or, if not fair, then at least logical – I was a 9 a.m. beer type by then. My favourites had these little penguins on the cans. They looked exactly the same as the Penguin Books logo. As well as the drifts of cans themselves, I enjoyed wallowing in the irony of this, because, thanks to my love of the cans, the only thing I could produce were these crabby scuts of paragraphs that were also maybe just aphorisms about how drunk I was. I can't remember them: I remember thinking, though, that I was embracing the fragmentary nature of literary form and its mimesis of fragmentary subjectivity in the era of late capitalism – or, at least, trying to think that I thought I was embracing such fragmentariness, when in fact I was a buckled fucking mess lying shirt open on a couch that neither she nor I owned. If I look back at it, the surprise is of course not that she left me: the surprise is that she let me into that apartment to begin with, and that she moved out, rather than kicking me out.

Brasília had been nothing but bardo time for me. I saw my months there as a tableau, two or three images moving towards stillness, nothing advancing, nothing changing: oxide-red earth, savannah nowhere, cicadas gone hoarse outside, while, inside, weeds push apart the tiles of an apartment that was new when we moved in here, profuse green sprigs taking over the grouting, a clump in the dampest corner whose twigs recalled the hollow thighbones of birds and crumbled when I poked at them. Fifteen floors down and a block away, from around a pool whose fat turquoise sloshing I could watch from where I sat, a bunch of kids dressed like Dwight Yoakam and June Carter whooped as a song they loved came up on the big speakers. This whole place felt as if it could be gone in a minute and the land wouldn't notice. Red dirt billowed in all day, collected in little comets around the pegs at the base of my chair, tacked to rubber strips edging the screen door, a red carpet of dead time waiting to roll out across everything. What possessed the Dwight

Yoakam and June Carter kids to put on their pool party that day is unknown to me. The clouds had been baling in for days, B-52 big and grey, with matching B-52 thunder-rolls for hours, and now it all began to dump down. The roundabout's red clay pie-shape got so saturated as to melt and flow in a violent, unbroken tide that sloshed up the steps of the luxury apartment I could see and envy from my two feet of balcony. I toasted the damage with a bottle of Sancerre and my girlfriend's cat, Piaf, freaked out at how loud my laugh was and sprinted off. The rain filled its usual tracks, signing its name deeper and deeper each time. The puddles were like vast inkblots. The red clay drank every mark. A ripped cable lay rat-tailed across what passed for the pavement. The red clay caked in the pores of a concrete lamppost, painted from within by its own sclerosis. On the building sites the workers would look in at the flooded trenches, the watery cement, and simply shrug, then start up a raucous poker game in the unfinished underground car park.

The day she left, I looked over at the Elis Regina poster on the floor under its pane of cracked and broken glass. My girlfriend had worn that exact same outfit – flower crown, pink boa, scoop-cut black dress – to the only con-cert of hers I'd ever seen, at a bistro in the centre of the city somewhere. A few songs in a mostly nude homeless lad known to the restaurant had wandered out of the hedges around the terrace, his face cratered and florid, his voice a rusted howl as he sang along. His performance had ultimately led to her abandoning the stage.

I went and sat on the tiny balcony, watching the world reel under the stun of the rain and the Dwight

Yoakam and June Carter kids running, shrieking, from around the swimming pools towards the palm-leaved shelter of the palapas. The new developments were draped with long gauzy veils that read 'Brookfield'. The man who ran the showroom van for this deluxe place would retreat into the fake living-room replica in the back trailer, feet up on a beige footstool, fingers steepled in his lap, rocking gently back and forth in the soft oxblood pleasure of his office chair. Cardboard boxes were melting to a brown slick. Bubble-wrap lay in the muck, looking octopus-suckery. Saplings poked up broken-umbrella shapes from the rubble at the base of my building. A mewl reached me from inside, then the thud of a tiny headbutt against the glass: Piaf, the cat. She scratched the glass. The sound spread a white pain star behind my eyes. 'I heard you the first time,' I said, and slid the door open. She scampered out to me, peered up from the corner, eyes huge, body braced, ready to flee if she had to. She looked a lot like my ex did before the end. She'd be crying at something I'd shouted, tiny hands to her face. Her fingers made me think of otters' claws, the same ones as on the videos she used to like on Instagram, the ones with all the squeaking that hurt my head and stopped me being able to concentrate at work. The cat gazed up, cowering and big-eyed. 'It's only me,' I said, even though it was me that was the problem. I'd gone too far the day before, cuffed her full in the jaw because she'd ripped apart an enormous dragonfly, left the strews lying everywhere. Then I'd walked out and stepped on a fish head lying on the tiles. 'Look.' I got up and crossed the floor, crunching bits of strewn dragonfly under my bare feet, and clattered a metal bowl onto the floor. I tipped out dry food. 'Truce.' Cotton mouthed, I went to the sideboard to tip instant coffee into yesterday's mug, stir in cold water, load in sugar, dose the goop with cognac from the depleted bottle on the counter.

This was another one of the brownout days, electricity wise, but the coffee wasn't bad cold, once the concoction had gotten me where I needed to be. The caffeine was for the vasoconstriction and the alcohol was to slow the coffee buzz away from the edge of paranoia, which was where the weed fug tended to land me these days. I took the cup out to the balcony and sat on the one Acapulco chair that Piaf hadn't wrecked with her claws, shooing her away from a frayed string as I did so. She hopped into my lap. I propped my feet on the crate of luxury wines, in a parody of the trailer-guy. When the man she left me for brought the thing over, he'd been sweaty, triumphant, plucking at his stupid fucking goatee, his hands trembling too much to light his cigarette, rattling off dollar-prices, *That Sancerre right there, that's three hundred bucks*, and the tired way my girlfriend had said, 'That's great, baby' to him and not me, that should have alerted me, probably, insofar as I could be alerted to anything. But I was the one drinking my way through them now, wasn't I. 'So, now who's laughing, eh, Piaf?' I said, jogging her on my knee, even though I knew the answer was probably her, and the laugh was probably a laugh of relief.

The lights came back on with a *thoom*. I opened my laptop. I put on videos of Neil 'Razor' Ruddock telling stories about when he'd played for Liverpool in a Sarf London tobacco wheeze. I laughed sometimes, along with him, even if I was too zoned out to keep track of what he was talking about. Cantona was involved, somehow. The video ended. The loading circle turned on the screen. It kept turning. I kept watching. It kept turning. I put on another one when I could pull myself out of the trance. I just wanted ambient human noise. The videos drowned out the all-over body sweats, the scalp prickles, the heat like a lamp under your skin turned way up, the shakes, the shivers, the nosefizz, the full, blurry eyes, that overwhelming sense of a small child's helpless tearfulness.

But I knew too that you can walk it off: you can tire it out, that sudden racing burn inside, stippling across the blood. The night walks had been good. Ache reddened the balls of my heels, pulsing up along the arches, same as those Brasília nights when I was keyed up enough to trek out and score later than was prudent to do so, when I headed out under a towering sky the livid blue-purple of an aubergine. Where I lived was a mix of new tower blocks that shone the gleaming black of a pristine iPhone and improvised housing for the people who were building and servicing those towers. On the edges the towers weren't as good: tussocky squares of grass and mud, banjaxed electric poles, falling-apart pavements, red mud for miles and miles, and then the same nothing as there'd always been stretching out beyond the last of them. Not one tile of the place was older than 2005. Not even the dirt had history: millennia of dead fruit and river muck, some of it solid, most of it not. The only stones banded with fossil-life were in chunks of marble imported for someone's kitchen island. Heading out at night, I'd walk along the edges of steep canyons between the tower blocks over paths of raw dirt, dried cement-spills, fluorescent signs on stakes offering unfinished apartments for sale. When it rained, the big strafes of wind would swing out of nowhere and make the unwindowed sockets of the new towers howl like hungry dogs. Between them, an infinite vista of boredom that humbled all these sushi-restaurants, burger-bars, in-earnest eighties-themed nightclubs. I'd walk past handcuffed people at the Metro station and duck the turnstile because the cops were too busy haranguing the people they'd cuffed. The new skeleton of the Mané Garrincha stadium gleamed in the moonlight. The buildings of the centre flitted past through bluish anytime-anywhere phosphene glare, as clean and sterile as the interior of electronics. Barely see-ing these buildings at all was the best way to see them. The lull of the train's forward motion and the dullness of the view made me nod out and dream of trying to run through an airport terminal full of Irish gift shops: plush green hoodies, teddy bear shamrocks, beer mats and coasters showing Clonmacnoise and Jerpoint Abbey and the Giant's Causeway, while the travelator below my feet whumped and rippled and started to flow back-wards, against my sweaty jogging.

The Metro jerked to a halt at the final stop, waking me, and I got up and wiped my mouth with the back of my hand and headed through the Rodoviário feel-ing as though I'd been uploaded into an MS-DOS game, everything around me simply mobile blocks moving smoothly over plane oblongs. Up high, near the top floor of the bus station, a woman sat on a paused escalator with her chin resting on the spread parentheses of her hands, knees up to her chin, watching the advertisements loop around, shapes of heated plasma in a mad neon toss. I walked along a footbridge, above a sixteen-lane highway, while a modernist church and a seventies-build shopping centre caught blue and crocus-yellow tints from the sky, followed by row after row of towers covered in bronze glass that made them look like the embossed leather bindings of old encyclopaedias; the ocean crash of the traffic washed up over me. I don't remember any pavements: just undulations of grass parching on that rich, oxide-red earth. Fat white cumulus bobbed over me. I had a desert inside my body; the feeling was spreading a dry yellow fog through me. The slow chop of water in the reflecting pools by the Congresso Nacional recalled faulty game graphics.

The sun was going down. The people who hung out here late at night were a lot like me, in that they were on heavy drugs much of the time, stumbling around dazed on the tracks worn in the grass. There weren't any squares to linger in, not many buildings you could sleep outside where the cops wouldn't hassle you. Away from the main roads, there were still plenty of towers. There was the plink of the aircon, the buffeting of black sacks over broken vents as they plumped and ballooned into the night, wrinkles catching the light. I saw some of the other people who either didn't have homes or didn't want to be there craning their heads and picking along with a kind of holy slowness, an expression on their faces as though they were privy to some revelation I wasn't able for: their smiles deeper than the manic ones looking down at us from the hoardings.

A guy rattled past in a copper wheelchair that looked twice my age, holding a Phillips-head screwdriver in one hand and a plea scrawled on a scrap of cardboard propped up in his lap. The guy in the wheelchair blanched and pulled back from me when I said 'Hi', clutching the screwdriver harder, muttering, looking at me as though he could tell me things about my face that I wouldn't want to know. Another walked along just fine as he wielded a padded crutch, giving it a real sabre swish and stab, a big sore grin on his face.

I made for the bus stop. All I had to do was stand there slapping at the mosquitoes that were there and at the mosquitoes that were not until someone sidled out of the mango trees with an offer. The menu would follow whether I said anything or not. Mostly I'd get crack, which I didn't get much out of, or a crap injectable heroinlike syrup that had been stood on about as many times as there were miles between here and the border with Venezuela. The real stuff went to São Paulo and Buenos Aires and Montevideo: all we got here was a trickle. I assume the rates I got for it were extremely bad, but it's a false economy to try to negotiate, or shop around, or head off into the undergrowth, because you might leave your phone or your bank card or even your shoes behind you there. Knowing me I would sooner live without shoes than make a pointless dent in my drug budget; in short, this would only mean further expenses, such as cutting my feet walking on stones, those cuts getting infected, then the foot getting gangrene. So, getting ripped off would actually save me money. Whenever I hear people share at meetings about all the times they've been beaten up trying to score or being mugged shortly after scoring or whatever similar calamity, I feel mystified that none of this ever happened to me. I am not tall, I am not strong, I wear glasses. I do not give off a streetwise impression. The only danger I'd pose in a fight would be if I was smushed to bits and someone jabbed themselves by accident on a jut of bone. Other people's tales of violence leave me baffled. If I am perfectly honest, the people I bought from were nice – perhaps because I was so easy to overcharge, perhaps because I was so desperate and smiley and let them be quick. I'd go home with my hand cupped around the baggie in my pocket feeling as if I'd slipped away with the fire in a fennel stalk, my excitement turning the growth of plantlife beyond the buildings into a seethe of tapehiss that nobody else could hear.

One of the nights the bus got a flat and I had to walk the rest of the way home. I didn't mind. I had drugs. Their presence gave me such equanimity. I had a dab of my baggie for the long trek back, turned the night into the interior of an opal, an enticing tunnel of darkness and glitter. This was all I needed, all anyone needed, a warm foggy feeling inside and outside, and gently flowing colours to look at for so long that it felt like the colours were moving through my veins. There was nothing to anything, simply a flat onward motion, on and on through the too-warm night. It was just me and the ochre and orange palette of the electriclit night and the sameness of it all every which way as far as the eye could see. After a while, though, the relentless sameness scorched me in a panic that turned my fingers and toes into floating white streamers, while some unseen hand stuffed clots of vegetation down my neck, but another dab on the gums was enough to turn that fear into vague tingle that I then felt able to call by another name.

When I got back in, the security guard I liked talking to was sitting out front at the foot of the building in an office chair. She was nice. She knew I got high and she knew my girlfriend had left me, so she let me get high in a quiet nook away from the security cameras. New arrivals in a place always think they're so original, trying to find their own outdoor nooks. But you'll never be the first to find a clearing, especially in a city with so much soft grass and so many mango trees. There'll always be someone waiting for you – a bunch of lads wearing bits of phone cables as bracelets and fanning themselves with torn-off cardboard, or chucking stones up at the mango trees to bring down a fat one, or lying propped on their elbows against stacks of faded magazines, philosophers lounging on the edge of the agora – philosophers who've decoded that map which leads beyond thought, beyond speech; philosophers who've made an evanescent poem of their own lungs, their own veins; philosophers who've figured out too much too fast, who have seen too far and too deeply, who've understood that whatever system you could invent with language is a mesh that sizzles to ash on contact with any true light, and that the only truth is that fall which is indistinguishable, at the level of sensation, from the sensation of flight. The small talk of these philosophers will be boring at first, then annoying, then pleading, but a strange kind of pleading, the kind that suggests you'll lose what you're asked for if you don't give it freely. It is simply too stressful. No: if you have a safe place to bang up, boring as it may be, you're better off going there; why not lie down, sun yourself, become an iguana. No picturesque experience is worth maybe losing your shoes. So, I sat down on the empty office chair beside the security guard and got my baggie out like it was a pack of cigarettes.

'What're you reading tonight?' I said to her, knocking ash out of my pipe.

'Saramago,' she said, marking the page with her finger and shutting the book to show me its cover: a scribble of black chalk on a teal background. 'You ever pick this one up?'

'Not yet,' I said.

'He has a bit at the end where the guy sees a zeppelin flying over the café he's sitting in,' she said. 'It has a swastika on it. And the zeppelin's flying to Latin America, he says. And it's true, it's real, I looked it up. They flew zeppelins with swastikas carrying letters for Brazil and Argentina and Paraguay and everywhere.'

'Did they ever stop?' I said, and licked shut the paper of the cigarette I was rolling. 'You know. Metaphorically, or whatever.'

'It's a good point,' she said.

She wasn't noticeably tough or anything, but she'd told me about the place where she lived, out in Taguatinga, and it sounded a tough neighbourhood. The only other person I'd met from there was this smiley shaven-headed Evangelical kid at my friend's baby's christening. He was in the armed response unit of the police force and didn't want to talk about any of it. At the front of the security guard's house, she'd told me, was an immense lilac and turquoise LED key that pulsed all night above a locksmith's booth. Her bed was at the back, shaded by the swaying leaves of rubber plants and banana trees, a hood of green light that soothed the glare through her window.

Sometimes when I was high enough I got lost in a headspin of pure yellow sunlight and humid womby gloom. Drugs were so cool. You just became this rain of particles that fell into another person's life and then you weren't in yours anymore. It was better than being a writer. I was already a better writer than anyone I knew by being able to do this, and even better again by not having to bother writing in order to do it. The needle was a kind of 'Pen-Nib 2.0', making me a brave disruptor.

A whoop came up through the air from the underground car park of the building site across the road, and somebody turned the volume up.

'I can't stand those guys,' I said, shaking my head.

'They're actually pretty respectful,' said the security guard. 'It's their bosses I can't take.'

'I hear that.' I unrolled the sheet of foil across my lap.

'Anyone with any kind of money at all is furious these days,' said the security guard. She had her head back and was scratching under her chin. 'They'll have their generals back in power yet.'

'Thought I was living in the future when I first saw this place,' I said. The towers gleamed black in the night above the undulations of the flatlands.

'I mean you kind of are,' she said. 'In that it's just going to be generals and malls from here on in. Arts students gouging each other with bike spokes for the last packet of chips in the machine. That kind of thing.' She licked a finger and turned the page. I preferred it when she talked like this. Sometimes she'd talk about the Old Testament and get a bit whacked out, doing her own riffs – the factories' smoking altars of brick, the Tree of Life being the tree shapes inside the lungs, the providential plot a big mess seen up close because we were so limited, but that confusion, that lack of knowledge, that was essential for God's plot to unfold. He wanted us to have no eyes to see and no ears to hear and to keep moving along inside the thudding walls of that great body of his. An organ, she said, does its best work when it doesn't know it's an organ. If the heart stopped to think, well, then the heart would stop, wouldn't it, and then where would you be. It was only the people who fell out who were lost and damned, she'd say, but that was OK, because it was actually quite hard to fall out. At least that's what I remember her telling me. She could have told me anything and I'd probably remember it that way.

'Nice night,' I said, letting fall my cigarette.

'It is,' she said.

And then I took up my glass pipe and got out my blowtorch lighter and listened to the low roar of it for a moment, before setting off to chase those colour-of-dried-blood trails over the wrinkles and ridges of the foil, the towers glittering around me, the trees pocking the flatlands beginning to sway in a wind I couldn't feel. Smoke rose in a slow bolus, the head of an octopus amid wavering tentacles. The blood hummed in my cheeks.

As for heroin, I bought my first bag of the stuff down-stairs from my apartment in Barcelona, in a little bar that occupied the bottom floor of my building. I had just dropped out of my PhD programme and was tak-ing an English teacher-training course in the city. The plan from there was to go to Brasília, to see my girl-friend, whom I'd met in Dublin. I was living on some money left to me by my grandfather to do all of this. But the money felt cursed to me, burning coals that I needed to chuck out of my pockets before they left black scorches all over my skin, scorches with a soft centre, one I could insert a finger into, push all the way through to the bone, or into whatever tender organ lay beneath. I'd had that money sitting in my account since my grandfather's death in 2002, when I was fourteen. At that time, he hadn't changed his will in twelve years; a will which he'd made at a time when one of his four sons hadn't been doing as well as the three others, and so he'd divided his fortune between his many grand-children and a son. My mother must have been hurt by this. It seemed to me she'd gotten so little out of that family. Her mother had been dying from 1972 or so, of emphysema, finally passing away eleven years later, after my mother's marriage to my father. Most of that intervening decade, my mother spent by her mother's side, and my father would remember a lot of their dates taking place in the must of that bedroom, too. I could see the red drapes, the thick light, smell the tang of ethanol, see the dim gleam on brown glass bottles. Her death was slow and painful. She was too ill to even make it to the wedding. When my mother and father went to see her en route from the reception, she'd said, 'What took you so long to get here?'

My mother told me she felt a kind of vertigo then, a pit that had opened, which she was falling endlessly backwards into. My father had held her by the shoulders. Four months later her mother was dead.

My mother says she felt like Cordelia in *King Lear*, that she felt like the girl in The Beatles song 'She's Leaving Home'. She watches clip shows of news from the 1980s and tells me that the stress and darkness of that decade on screen were matched by the stress and darkness of that decade in her life. I see her in my head then.

She used to spend her evenings sobbing as the anniversary of her mother's death on 14 July approached. She was often a volcano rumbling and readying to blow, sucking the air into a spiral, readying to huff out dense bundles of grey smoke and a vermicular spackle of ash over everything. She'd cry like she was trying to hock some enormous solid out of her body, but it wouldn't budge. Her mouth made a gargling sound as though she'd been stuffed to the thrapple with ceramic chips. I heard this same crying at the funeral home in Bagenalstown, my grandfather in the coffin under pinkish light.

His death at eighty-four had been sudden. Right to the end he had been hale, tall, garrulous, with a deep, phlegmy laugh – the smile never off his face, his barrel chest huge, his medicine-ball paunch straining against shirt and braces while my mother and father brought him plates of food during Sunday dinners at our house. I'm still not sure how he died. Some blame a badly cleaned jacuzzi. Another theory runs that he died after abusing herbal health remedies. The third, simplest, maybe truest: he pushed himself too hard on too cold a morning, had a heart attack after a hill walk.

This can't be how it happened, but I remember my mother approaching the coffin, taking the glasses from his face, and folding them into her pocket. The air is salmon tint and thickens liquidly around her and a hush falls as she crosses the floor to take her father's glasses from his face, then she walks backwards, folding shut the glasses, moving through a silence that's now more of a hush with a buzz around it, and the buzz rises as she steps backwards to find my father's hands on her shoulders, back into a gesture, a signifier of normality, and the impossibly filmic smoothness of this dreamed memory of mine – played and replayed so many times that no possible truth element could remain, so static-fuzzed and distortion-futzed has that head-tape become – can end, and the real, or what passes for the real, pick up again. They'd ushered us out then so they could screw the lid down on my grandfather. The darkness outside smelled coldly of petrol fumes and chimney smoke. I could hear the whine of the drill and the thudding judder of the screws against the pale wood.

When the will came out, I assume it had hit her as the final confirmation that family was nothing but a black hole to her, that the insults would never end. When I'd withdrawn that money from the Post Office, aged twenty-three, ready to run away, I stumbled out of the bank after authorising the transaction feeling like I'd broken out of jail. My head reeled. The Gothic building behind me with its verdigris cupola and weather-vane felt too on the nose. Even though the money was technically mine, it still struck me as stealing: the present robbing from the future, maybe; me robbing from family, definitely. I'd have to punish myself with it, or use it as fuel to propel me as far away as possible, somewhere I wouldn't punish myself as though I'd committed a crime.

*

I'm not the only one in my family to use escape as a tactic. A paternal uncle made a break for Spain as soon as he could at the age of nineteen. He's barely Irish anymore. I love this about him. He's ruddy and effusive and his English is deckle-edged with the sounds of his adopted language: short vowels, percussive consonants, long 's'-runs that turn whole sentences into one breath.

After I ran away, to Barcelona, I took a long train trip to see him, through landscapes smooth as a seabed: worn-down Armorican foldings. Closing in on the station, I went to stand between the carriages, letting the wind beat me about the head. During my visit, his teenage years came blooming up.

'Your father helped me,' he said. 'Helped me so much.'

He showed me a photo on his phone: himself in 1980. Skinny leather tie, feathered Hall & Oates hair. He looks up at the camera with a sceptical, pursed mouth and cagey eyes.

'Imagine trying to get away with that in your grandfather's house,' Kevin told me. 'No hitting – just a lot of silences. I would come into the kitchen and he would stop talking. Really obvious stuff like this – addressing me through my sisters. "Tell your brother to do this, tell your brother not to do that" kind of thing. Someone told your dad this was getting to me. He had moved out by then, was married to your mother. He brought me for a drive one day. I don't remember that we said much. At one point, out of nowhere, he said: "It's OK to hate your father." He turned in his seat checking I had heard him. Then he dropped me home. I knew I could run away then.'

On the table lay a plate of jamón ibérico. Blackfoot pigs roaming forests, feeding on acorns. Calcium traces stay in the meat: white dents, white streaks; comet heads, comet trails. I ate none of it: I haven't eaten meat in years.

My uncle showed me around his whole region. I wanted to inhale his words about how he had gotten there: I needed a manual for getting out and staying out. 'Basically, Vegas for the Romans,' he told me when we visited the wrecked amphitheatre outside his town. The undersea look of ruined stone, the empty sockets where marble plating was tugged free and sold. Deep in the wreck, where gladiators waited for their bouts, the air was cold, heavy and smelled vaguely of rivers.

We drove to a museum. Through the car window I could see grass the colour of oxides and sulphides. The museum floor was plate glass over an old temple floor. I thought of coral. In the rows of coins on display I saw how the dynastic noses and chins swapped across generations. One explanatory text said how alcohol was used to clean some of them, a clear burn that seared away dirt scabs, patina. In the floor I watched the caught reflections of clouds crumble in over the hills.

The next room over held a statue of Aeneas. His son hadn't made it through – his right arm ended in a broken stub – but his father remained, battened tight to his back. I remember Aeneas's stricken, noseless face and his heavy kilt made of small, ticket-stub-shaped chevrons of stone etched with the faces of gods. I couldn't figure the caption out: 'FOUND IN A CONTEXT OF DESTRUCTION. The statue is believed to have survived because of hidden structural imperfections in the ruin where it was located.'

When we pulled in at a café for a pitstop the clouds were swagging low and volcanic over the hills. Over our coffees I looked at the rib of black stone that arced across the hills. I thought of the skeletons of whales.

'It's OK to hate your father,' I said to my uncle. 'Big words.'

'Yours is pretty good, in fairness,' said my uncle.

I let my mind's eye move over the statue: the missing nose, the empty eyes, the upturned face and missing child, the anguish.

'He's a lot more than that,' I said.

*

Barcelona's mood fit mine, green and red and yellow lights making enigmatic spill shapes on wet pavements, the wine and the drugs and the exhausting walks I'd take which hollowed me out to a cardboard cutout. I went to late showings of seventies thrillers at old porn cinemas. I walked around all night. Everything felt urgent, even though nothing was happening. My life was all setting, no plot, no character, all selfhood reduced to a white bead of moisture skittering across the hot ceramic of a stove. But that feeling never lasted, and by the time I had gotten to the end of my course in Barcelona, the sensation of freedom had drained away entirely and reverted to panic. I'd gotten out, alright, but too far out, and now I was stood there frozen in the dazzle and vertigo of a freedom I had no idea how to use.

On dim days like these, where I couldn't do anything but sit on the corner of my bed feeling the feverish slickness of my forehead slowly drip down the bridge of my nose, it was as though I hadn't even left Dublin at all. I'd be sure I was still sitting in the coffin-tight wood panels of the pub nearest the campus, the one where I'd go alone after the library closed, the night slowly blurring into one enormous stout-black river carrying me away into nothing. I pretended there was a kind of chaos zen to how I was living, to the insight I'd had into the paralysing nature of freedom, and how the drugs were the real freedom, with their lucid, moment-by-moment sensation of smooth golden cruise inside, but that's not true – it was just the relief of feeling my own panic momentarily drowned into silence. I couldn't tell if the cricket shirr was really that loud, or if it was because the electric wires crossing past my window were frayed almost past use, or if it was my actual neurons buzzed to hell by my panicked chase along the back alleys of the Barri Gòtic in search of drugs. The money needed to be out of my body as quickly as possible – the deep berries and acid cut of Merlot, the snowy lilac expanses that Malbec opened in my palate, the sudden, scudding hit of Shiraz, its sucking depths. I'd skip dinner entirely, eating nothing after twelve noon or so. The wine hit harder that way. There were ways to defeat hunger other than food. The sleepiness and serenity of the drink could do instead of peace, instead of food, instead of anything I wanted, really: skipping meals as strategy, a way of kicking the can of hunger down the road, saving me a couple of euro a day, I supposed, if I added it up, and converted into all this pellucid and easy-on-you time, a jacuzzi wallow, with the side benefit of making me quite good with money, all things considered.

The downstairs bar where I bought the heroin had a Vietnamese name that's lost to me, if I ever even had it. The walls were decked with photos that showed rags of fog tearing against pine-studded crags, terraced fields, winding mountain pathways, lonely cottages overlooking valleys. There was a courtyard of beige gravel and dead acacias out the back. This, I thought to myself, as I sat down with my sweating caña at one of the metal tables, was the true deep feel of Europe. I picked at a flake in the paint with my nail. I was close enough to the door to see inside, to where an old TV was showing Barcelona pasting Getafe or someone. The young couple who ran the bar leaned on the copper, smoking and speaking in a language I didn't recognise. After a while a man of around fifty shambled in the door, with a salute to the young couple. Even though it was a hot day, he was wearing a dirty mac open over a white shirt that had begun to yellow. The man behind the bar shook his hand, while the woman just nodded, her arms folded, looking a little concerned. The man in the raincoat saw me in the courtyard and pointed, as though asking their permission to go through. The woman looked at the TV. Her boyfriend or husband nodded a little over-eagerly. I watched the man come towards me, issuing me the same salute.

'Buenas tardes,' he said, as he neared my table. He had a bundle of scratch cards hanging from one hand. His pockets were stuffed with postcards that showed dribbly ink and watercolour pictures of the Sagrada Família and the Casa Batlló and Parque Güell and so on, except there were human faces growing out of all of the lines, and the ink in which they were drawn was so watery that the bright colours made me feel afraid of him.

'No hablo español,' I said. This was untrue: I'm a quick learner, and I like languages. I just wanted to get rid of this guy who seemed to be some kind of hawker. 'Perdón.'

'Oh, that's quite alright,' he answered in an English that had a BBC edge to it. 'May I?' And he pulled out a chair.

He had a tingling sound rising from him, that high tintinnabulation you get when a lightbulb is about to burn out, and the noise almost had a smell, a mosquito smell: that's how my head described it.

He sat down opposite me, but didn't take off his coat. I could smell the sweat from him – that orangey shut-in-all-day tang, the kind I recognised from my own pores.

'I don't really want to buy these, though,' I said, and pushed the scratch cards towards him. 'I'm not from Spain. So, if I won I couldn't claim them.'

He chuckled. 'Oh, I'm not selling them.'

The guy who ran the bar was approaching, carrying an espresso on a saucer. Raincoat Man collected it and thanked him, then thanked him again as the guy took a battered white envelope from under his arm and handed this over as well.

'Ah, qué maravilla,' said Raincoat Man, wagging the envelope in thanks. It looked heavy.

Raincoat Man pulled the top off a sachet of sugar and poured it into his cup. He watched me watching him, smiling with one side of his mouth. The light was picking out flecks of grey in the spots he'd missed while shaving.

'*Star Trek*,' he said.

'I don't follow, chief.'

'How I learned English,' he said. 'From watching *Star Trek*.'

'Cool.' I lifted my glass. I felt a horrible, doomed pressure landing on me. These were the only people I was ever going to meet. I'd begun my social life wanting to meet writers. Now I was just bouncing around with the dregs, the roaches, in the mesh of a gutter.

'Salud,' he said. 'Or, should I say, *sláinte*.'

'Oh, very good. Very good.'

Raincoat Man picked up the scratch cards and fluttered them with the edge of his thumb, shaking his head.

'The forgeries get lazier every year. Look.' He picked at the edge of the silver square that you were meant to scratch off. The whole square lifted off in one go. 'Cheap, cheap.'

'Well spotted.'

'Yes.' He stroked the side of his neck as though it hurt, then sipped his coffee. 'You know, I've seen you.'

'Oh yeah?' I felt a sinking in my blood.

'Yes. Up on your balcony.' He mimed sucking on a joint. 'A bit of this, no?'

A clammy chill crept up the back of my neck.

'I haven't a clue what you're talking about. I just arrived.'

He tutted and swatted the air with his hand.

'Oh, please, don't give me these preliminaries. I'm not going to arrest you. I just want to save you a little money, that's all.' He reached into his raincoat pocket and dropped a small plastic bag of something that looked like soil on the table. 'How much do you spend on marijuana per week? Roughly.'

'Not a huge amount.'

'But probably still too much. The notorious precio de extranjero, no?'

'It is what it is. I'm not from here, after all.'

'Yes, well.' He nudged the bag towards me with the tip of one finger.

'Give me fifty for that,' he said.

'I don't really do powder drugs,' I lied, because I'd often snorted stuff at college parties without really knowing what it was – up or down, it didn't matter the direction, or even the velocity, so long as I was heading out of myself.

He gave a one-shoulder shrug, his face suddenly sad. He tutted again, then took a scuffed laminate that showed his grinning face with the word Policía underneath and said, 'Well, let's make sure, shall we? With a little look around your home.'

The chill on my neck turned to heat. The badge might be no more real than the scratch cards, but I couldn't know that. I wanted to call him a cunt, but all I did was hold his gaze, shake my head and take out my wallet. I peeled off the fifty meant to last me for that week's food and forked it over between my index and middle fingers.

'Much obliged,' said Raincoat Man, and promptly pocketed the money. He drained his cup. 'Like I said, I saved you some money.' He got to his feet, tapped beside the baggie, then said, 'Now put that away and have a fine evening.'

I looked at the baggie on the table for a moment, trying to figure out how I was supposed to feel. There was a steam-hot panic rushing in and out of my pores with every breath. I figured I'd be in trouble if I saw this guy again. I had no idea if he was a type, or if he was bluffing, but it'd be the last time I went to that bar, I told myself, and that cooled the panic down a bit. But under those two feelings there was something else, a crawling, dark sort of a sensation, something picking in and around the gaps between my ribs, on dainty pointed scorpion feet, and that was the part of me that was glad I'd spent fifty quid on a load of old mud that had probably been stepped on about a dozen times between Afghanistan and here. I had an excuse if I took it now. Buying it had been for the greater good, and now, if I got fucked up on it, I wouldn't be drinking so much: so, essentially, I'd be saving money, just as the cop had said. I swept the baggie into the inner pocket of my leather jacket with the palm of my hand. It was probably too warm to be wearing leather, but I never felt the warmth anymore – I was too thin, too trembly, and the pallor of my face wasn't the kind that got suntanned away. I watched the man go, the tails of his raincoat bouncing a little in the draught of his walking. The young woman behind the bar didn't take her glare from his back, while her boyfriend exhaled heavily in relief and leaned on the copper countertop. I drank off my second beer and brought the two glasses back in.

'I'm really sorry,' the man running the bar said.

'Who was that?'

'It doesn't matter,' he said.

'A cop,' the woman said. 'A bad one. Don't think about him again.'

'I'll try,' I said, then left, heading back upstairs to the apartment.

I dropped the bag of heroin on the plastic table on the balcony and looked at it for a while, rubbing at my mouth. Below, some teenagers were breakdancing to remixes of old classic soul songs while a syrupy-orange sun went down, igniting the windows. I went inside for my laptop, looked up *easy ways to take heroin*, then got a sheet of foil from the drawer, a toilet-roll tube from the bin, and settled down with the fullest of the cigarette lighters that I kept buying and losing. The powder sputtered and became a thick, potent-smelling rivulet whose feeling in my body made me shiver the way the basslines rising from the speakers on the square outside thumped within me. I put on 'Cortez the Killer', turned up the speakers and lowered my face to the toilet-roll tube and the toilet-roll tube to the heroin. My veins felt smoked, all rust-coloured in there, ashy flakes of cinders turning over and over. My body swayed, back and forth, back and forth: kelp in a laketide.

Once I'd gotten that first purchase out of the way, I found it absurdly easy to buy heroin. I'd go tottering around the sadder edges of the Barrio Gòtic, brown gloomy streets where a canopy of washing swayed overhead and the windows burbled with TV stations in all the languages of the world. There were colonnades where men would lean with their backs to the sun-warmed pillars and give backward nods and little thumbs-ups, hissing 'Hashish? Coca?', and that'd be it; I'd just have to say 'Y qué más?' and the offer would not be long about coming. A couple of weeks later, I injected for the first time.

Back when I'd lived in Dublin, when I'd volunteered on Fridays with the soup run for homeless people, I'd worked with another guy. He disappeared for a few weeks. When he came back one week, looking sheepish, he'd told me, in a low confidential voice, as he held open the tin of sugar for me to spoon some into a cup of coffee for a trembling woman in her forties, that he'd had a relapse, had had to get his head clear before he'd trust himself going outside with active drug users again.

'Did you feel awful?' I said, handing the cup across to the woman. We were standing beside the Daniel O'Connell statue just up from the bridge. A cluster of people was around us, waiting for soup, sandwiches, whatever we had.

'I do now,' he said, putting the lid back on. 'But that's just pride. Ego. All the time I'd built up clean, down the jacks. Maybe I needed to lose it to lose the ego and do it right this time.'

'Fair,' I said, counting out plastic-wrapped sandwiches, handing them to my friend so he could pass them out to the woman's kids.

'But at the time,' he said, 'I felt fucking superb.'

'How did you do it?'

'Wrapped myself up in a blanket, crawled in a wardrobe. Huffed away through a jacks-roll tube off of foil.'

'That doesn't sound too scary,' I said.

'Oh, it isn't,' he said. 'That's the problem.'

When he said that to me, it felt like someone stamping my passport.

*

The morning I first shot up was a rainy one. I had been told by the landlord that another tenant would be moving into the spare room. I fingered my current baggie, saw a little powder drop from the folds, clumping with the remains. She'd be tired when she arrived. She'd have a load of stuff with her. It felt imperative that she meet a friendly face at the door. This would require drugs. But there wasn't enough in the bag to merit snorting or huffing. I'd have to bang it up. It was force majeure. It wasn't my fault. It wasn't even my desire. Luckily I'd been thinking about it since that first time. I'd even picked up a pack of syrettes from the pharmacy. I'd been nervous but nobody had said anything. I supposed I could have been a tourist whose aged mother had diabetes or something.

As I uncapped the syrette, my legs were still stinging from the previous night's walk. I was floored in an amber mist that rose to my knees. Barcelona at night was the ear canals of some immense skull: these long, winding corridors of stone the colour of soap or bone, alleys that went on for ever, continuous with my skull, yet bigger than it, too. My head had been yattering at me. I'd tried to come down with an omelette sandwich and a milky coffee in an all-night cantina, but the tab had gotten its second wind and now it was my turn to be doing the jabbering, this time into the ear of a street performer from Mozambique who was waiting out the hours until the Metro started up again. He'd truss himself in pink feathers and fairy lights and stand on a Roland amp, singing Frank Sinatra songs. He got a bit of disability support from the government on account of his achondroplasia. The change people gave him rounded it out. I asked him if tourists ever did stuff to him, and he frowned.

'Do stuff to me?' he said.

'My friend has it too,' I said. 'Achondroplasia. He dresses up as a leprechaun. The English stag tours mess with him.'

'If anybody were to fuck with me in that way,' he said, in Spanish made silky by his Portuguese, then held up his hand as though he were cradling a goblet, then twisted. He let his gaze drift back to the football highlights. The bluish flicker of Messi passing to Xavi and Xavi passing to Iniesta and Iniesta passing back to Messi shimmered in the faux-marble surface of the counter. Messi put the ball in the net. The commentator reacted as though this had never happened before. The guy from Mozambique sucked in a deep breath, huffed it out, dropped some change in the tray and got off the stool.

'Have a good night,' he said and gave my knee a matey pat en route past me.

Caught in the rain on my way home, I'd stripped to my still-dry underpants and put on my long black coat over the top, a drenched sock pulled dripping over the fire alarm so I didn't set it off. I made myself a carajillo with the proportions reversed, and stood on my two feet of balcony, watching the dark mud flow in one violent, unbroken tide towards the deluxe building that I could see from my window. I toasted the flood. I hated the people living there. Their rooftop parties kept me awake at night – not with the noise, just with the envy burn that my life didn't look or smell like theirs. Mucky water slapped the glass, left little whorls that were in the same pattern as the whitish calcites veining the interior lobby's marble floor. The new developments were draped with gauzy veils with the names of the contractors on them, the ground pegged with stakes and fluorescent, exclamatory signs. I was up early. One of the people selling the lots was sitting inside the showroom-van, scrolling, yawning. As the muck washed past her she looked up, saw it was sweeping right by her, then turned her gaze back to her phone. The TV beyond her feet showed ads: anti-ageing cream, then orthodontics, then high-fibre low-cal energy bars – more life, more life, no more history, only more life. I enjoyed that memory-free, language-free look to things.

I hadn't written a thing in weeks. I lurked around Els Tres Tombs and saw Colm Tóibín there the odd time, but I never went near him. I'd messed up enough meetings with writers I respected, and I didn't even know what I might have wanted from him. In the pub, back in Dublin, after a reading of our student society he'd read one of my poems in a magazine that was lying around and told me he liked it, fixing his hooded gaze on me, saying, 'This is a serious piece of work.' I felt something crumble inside me. The next line would have to be a serious piece of work, too, and, if this work felt in some way exceptional to him, then it was also exceptional to me, in that most of what came out of me was utter dross. I didn't write another poem all that year. It wasn't his fault. I seemed to hate writing. Although I'd published a couple of poems in a small magazine, I'd been too drunk and scared to turn up to the launch. I had decided afterwards that this made me a kind of ink-shaped enigma on the margins, one that only needed the artistic gesture to articulate itself, and which saw in words like *community* or *reputation* nothing but a waste of time, or a craven cowardice that kept writers from their only real job, which was the next sentence, the next line, the next paragraph, but not even I felt that to be true all the way down. Really I was just scared of turning up and feeling myself suffocatingly one among many, all of us footnotes. Expression no longer interested me. After all, everything was expression: the titles given to Spotify and YouTube playlists, the clothes I wore, the consumer profile ghosted out by the shape of my spending. The only thing I wrote was a shameless attempt to linger in the atmospheres of films and books I liked, in order to feel as though the pain I was drawing on resided somewhere other than my own head and body: the fluorescent lights of police compounds, neon-lit skyscrapers, shimmering dots of light, against the vaguely noirish background of an imperial capital going to seed, slowly losing a siege against invaders who made multiple, small-scale incursions in jeeps and pickups borrowed from news reports on the wars in the Middle East and the police repressions of Latin America. I was trying to capture what I believed was the sheer boredom of apocalypse, where things end at first slowly, then all at once. This doesn't seem to be how it actually happens, but it is certainly how the collapse of addiction happens. In the background of my novel, Euripides' couple or friendship pair Orestes and his cousin Pylades were moving through this landscape, on a quest to track down their own author, who keeps them in existence, from all the way across the seas. They arrive at a stormy port, same as where Ovid ended up, except it's also a kind of ruined St Petersburg. They are tired of being alive. They find their existence to be a thin nightmare. They have been living out the same mania in dozens of languages for centuries. Their story keeps pulling them apart when all they want to do is buy a small house somewhere with cheap fruit and lots of sun, so they can wear Hawaiian shirts all year round, and feel heavy salt oblivion draw sealike over the sharp trash of their pasts. They want to find the author so they can tell him to please just stop. They track their author down to a hotel where he lies on a four-poster bed in a room where the wallpaper, patterned with close-ups of veins in medical footage, pulses, and where his burbling speech, as he lies addressing the ceiling, drips ink blots that morph and re-form as they strike the milk-white sheets. The author wears dark glasses and looks like if Nigel Terry had played James Joyce. He is clutching a walking stick on his chest; it has an ivory stag as the grip. They hear his groaning, his babbling, and they realise by what he says that they are figures from his nightmares. Orestes picks up a pillow, as if to smother him, but Pylades holds him back, saying there's no way to make the suffering go away, that their suffering will only change shape if they find happiness.

When I say I wrote this book, what I really mean is that I took its printed-out pages and then shredded them; I left them in a bucket for the rain to turn into mulch, until the ink of my corrections in biro had run off, collecting in a bluish guck at the bottom. This I would gather up in a syrette and let dribble onto dried sheets of the paper pulp, before leaving the rippled canvases to parch on the roof, the rain rewriting the runoff again and again and again. The only bit I enjoyed was the tearing up and cutting of the pages. I'd use a steak knife from the kitchen, loving the crunch of the breaking fibres, the crack of the twine bindings. Once the sheets of shredded paper had dried, they'd be a lagging of dried grey weed collected on a beach. I cut them into squares afterwards, using a box cutter. I could probably have framed them, but then the rough-edged threads and the flaky paper would have been sealed behind glass. Besides, I liked it when the wind destroyed them, blew them against the low wall around the edge of the terrace, dashed them to nothing, a kind of sand of language, wispy, destroyed, crawled with an almost-writing of ink. I'd stare at the bits then, feel them blow against my ankles. True writing was deletion. Only people stupid enough to break themselves to the harness of form failed to realise this. I felt very pure to myself. I'd gather up the mix of word-dust and hairs and insect husks and airborne gleet caught on the building's roof and collect them in little pill bottles or stamp them into layers: dried weed on a beach, fibrous, greyish dust. They had the gritty look of what's left after you cremate someone. Sometimes I thought of mixing the words with heroin, of shooting them; the spongy paper shreds reinflating in my blood, giving me an embolism. Cremation would be cheaper than burial as far as my family was concerned, I reasoned, so the bleached coral of my remains would take on the same nothing as this writing all around me, want and expectation burned out, cinders coating the floor of some immense skull, drifts that lifted and dropped in warm, unknowable winds.

Across the road, in an alcove on the wall of an old church, St Anthony stood, pressing a skull against his forehead. I tested the point of the syrette with my thumb. I was bored, but I was safe. Floods heaped along the kerb. I'd seen a video from Nogales, Sonora on the US–Mexican border, of wayward rivers carrying away cars, taco-stands, tarpaulins, jeeps. Everything was being deleted. That's what we were watching. Ever since I was three, I'd been watching countries collapse: Somalia, Bosnia, Kosovo, East Timor, Afghanistan, Iraq, Libya, Lebanon, Egypt, Syria, Venezuela. We now lived in the blur that accompanied the final vanishing. In a book picked up from the library when I was a child I'd read about the future's coming disasters: Ebola, earthquakes, floods, acid rain, famine. Now that I was in the midst of them, I saw that all I needed was to stay as high as possible and wait for it to be my turn. I'd read the *Nicomachean Ethics* in college; I'd learned how contemplation was the highest good a person could aspire to. There were a whole load of others first, obligations to society and stuff like that, and you were meant to scale the big endless slippery fucking ladder of them. But I'd skipped all of those, gone straight to the good stuff. As long as there was money in my account and the drugs were cheap, I didn't need the middle rungs. I could just chill on the top – Belacqua at the start of *Purgatorio*, lounging all leonine and lazy, watching white light ripple on waves the way I was watching sun on floodwaters, wait for the wave that had my name on it to rise over me, then bow to that wave as it drowned me.

I looked away from the waters. I didn't know what time the flatmate would get here so I might have to hurry. I took an old Nescafé jar filled with cool boiled water from the mini fridge. I washed my hands. I wiped down my spoon. I uncapped the syrette, looked down the tip. It was a little tunnel, one that led to an underground river. With the syrette I drew up a little water and let it dribble onto the powder. I'd nicked a large ornate spoon from a cantina. I'd also nicked a large lighter in the shape of a blowtorch from a shop that sold absinthe to idiots and whose employees were forever on their phones. I turned on the lighter under the wet powder. The lighter flame thupped and then hissed, dancing. The mix bubbled, turned a cosmic-latte colour. The needle filled with a backwards snore. I tightened the belt, wiped a cotton swab heated in the microwave over my veins to get them to stand up, then chose one that branched into the palm of my hand and slowly inched the needle in – a nick, a long slow sting, and then an all-over body shiver that broke me into streams of atoms, funnelling down and out of view, into that nowhere place nothing else before or since has ever gotten me to. It no longer scared me to be in my body. I was no longer even there. I was one at last with the black pool.

*

Towards evening, the doorbell rang. I looked at my wrist: a nothing mark, big as a mosquito bite. Nobody would notice, especially if I wore a watch, which I wouldn't, so I dabbed on disinfectant cream that smelled of the brand my mother'd smear on my knees, then capped the gob with a circular beige plaster.

I took the spare keys from the hook, opened the door, and saw a woman a little older than me standing there wearing a pink sweater that matched the massive Samsonite she was hauling. She seemed to jerk back from me a touch. I didn't blame her. I had run for the door, given myself a bad dose of the spins, and now I was swaying while I waited for them to fade.

'Hi,' she said. 'I'm supposed to move in here?'

'Well, hello there,' I said. The fluffs on her sweater moved in slow, blown skeins: sand chased into manes by wind.

'You. You going to let me in?'

'Oh. Yeah. Here. Let me drag that.'

'Thank you.' Her accent sounded American. As I took the handle I saw that she had a snake tattooed on the back of her hand, a nose-ring, a dyed blonde bob wrapped in a headscarf, and she was wearing a long tan trench coat with a big woollen scarf, even though it was warm out there.

'Do you need to sit down?' she said.

'Oh yeah, that'd be brilliant.' I flopped onto the edge of her bed. 'Jesus Christ.'

'Let me get you some water,' she said, and went up the hall to the kitchen.

'I should show you around,' I said, weakly, as she returned with a brimming San Miguel glass that I'd nicked from a pub.

'You should sit there for a bit, I think.'

'Yeah. I suppose. How are you anyway?'

'Fine. Long flight.' She sat down on the office chair by the desk.

'Yeah? From where?'

'Mexico,' she said.

'Ah. That's class. I'd love to go there. Do you mind if I smoke?'

'If you let me have one.'

'Yeah, alright.' I fiddled the box out of my coat pocket. 'Holiday?'

'I'm here for a conference. Geology.'

'Cool.'

'Family tradition,' she said with a shrug. She told me her name was Helen, because I'd failed to ask. She then told me about her father working for Pemex, how she'd go on trips with him up to Saltillo, in the north, how they'd gone walking through a canyon one Sunday, how she'd seen big crags stained all over with white flecks of calcite that looked like writing, how she'd looked deep into the splits within the grey rock, how her dad had told her that they were looking back through millions of years to when they'd all formed, how on top of the rocks were cactus with neon orange swirls running through the colours of their needles, and purple flowers blooming out the top of them, and how her father had said how the minerals in the water they took in gave their flesh and their needles and their flowers those colours, how this meant that nothing really disappeared, only changed its form. She had been thinking about this the whole way across to the far side of the canyon, to the lip on the other side, from which they'd looked down at what her father had told her was the vast floor of a long-gone sea.

'He works for the dark side, though,' she said.

I squinted, trying to figure out if she was being cryptic or if I was just in bits. 'Oh.'

'Yeah. Basically, he helps people smash up everything other geologists want to study, then burn anything that can't be smashed up. They're burning time. That's what they do. Everything, all of this' – she gave a backward nod at the view through the window – 'the smog, the exhaust fumes, the acid rain eating all of the buildings, it's all because they're digging big wet dark chunks of time up out of the ground and setting them on fire. The past choking the future. We've broken time with all of this combustion. Well. We. They. Them. The oil. The companies. You know.'

'Yeah,' I said. 'Yeah. Wow. When you put it that way, you know.'

'It's fucked,' she said in a clipped voice. 'Fuck, man, my English is going to sleep,' she said. 'You know where the coffee is?'

'Sometimes,' I said. 'Yeah.' I let a couple of seconds pass until the headrush faded, then told her to follow me to the kitchen. I went right to the fridge, took out a can for myself, remembered my manners, reached in for a second, offered it to her.

'Oh, that's OK,' she said, holding a hand up. 'I don't do that anymore.'

'That's cool,' I said, and started to mess around with the percolator until it was making the right kind of guzzling noise. I rubbed my breastbone. The gargle and snore of it sounded the way my breathing did some mornings, that slow, laboured suction: a soaked pair of bellows going in and out. The carafe started to fill.

'Your English is really good,' I said. 'How'd that happen?'

'My ex was a gringa,' she said. 'She never learned Spanish. She couldn't even say my name right. So, I just got used to saying my name was "Helen" to make it easy for her. Everyone calls it me now. Their English is horrible. Yours is nicer. Softer. And I lived there, too,' she said. 'The States, I mean. I transferred. Salt Lake City.'

'Salt Lake City, fucking hell. The beautiful people.'

A frown quivered across her eyebrows.

'All look like fascists to me, man,' she said, 'but whatever floats your boat. You know they all join the CIA afterwards? Those kids?'

'Which ones are those?'

'Oh, all of them, really.' She poked at her nose-ring with the pad of her thumb. 'But these ones were special.'

She told me how the noise and lights of police helicopters would wake her up in the early mornings. One morning, getting a bus, she'd looked up, seen parts of bodies hanging from the overpass. Sometimes she'd sit down at her work bench and a lab partner might come in with his face a smushed-up strawberry from the cops beating the shit out of him.

'You want to live when you're young,' she said. 'You want to live, whatever age you are. But everywhere I turned, no matter the time of day, no matter where I was, no matter who I was with, I was just seeing the violence everywhere.'

I watched the coffee brim to the surface.

'Shit,' I said.

'Yeah,' she said. 'Real shit.'

I flicked the switch off, poured her a cup, handed it across. Standing there, listening to her, my coat on over my underpants, the nap of it still soaked from last night's rain, I felt small. Mine was pretend chaos, pretend suffering, pretend intensity. There was a thrum of something not quite envy going through my blood. It could have been admiration, or maybe I just felt intimidated, but there was a hot beat to it that made the outline of my body more a billow of lines than a body per se. I imagined her life in the city, streets the same temperature as her blood, the whole huge map coded in her nerves, her synapses timed to its rhythm, surfing disjunctures, traffic-noise, the skirl of brakes, the judder of pneumatic drills, the sirens, everything that was cratering my head in the whole time. All I'd been doing was moping and killing time, both when I was aware of it and when I wasn't. I was a bucket of offal, nerve-and-tendon spaghetti spilling over the sides, gristle and gobbets and pucks of matter and shite: the books I hadn't been able to write, the poems I'd given up on mid-draft, the songs I'd half learned to play on the guitar before simply noodling around on the fretboard, waltzing slowly out of time, getting bored, leaving it down.

'We could go for a walk or something,' Helen said, rubbing her eyes. 'I'm trying to fight jetlag. They say you shouldn't sleep. You can show me around.'

'Yeah, why not,' I said. 'Although I'd say you know this place as well as I do.'

'I just got here.'

'Ah, I never remember where I end up.'

She was looking at me steadily. 'Is it a bit out of control?'

'What?'

'The' – she gave a chin-jut at the can I was drinking from – 'I saw the little bag,' she said. 'On your table. And little bags. Plural. On the floor.'

The floor went thin, fixed to open under my feet.

'Don't worry,' she said. 'It's OK. It'll take more than that to faze me.'

She reached into her pocket, took out keys that hung from a black keyring that had a gold circle on it, with the letters 'NA' embossed at the centre.

'Oh,' I said.

'I've got like seven years off everything like that,' she said.

'But you're like my age.'

'It got bad very young.' She pocketed the keys. 'So, you know, if it gets bad, you can ask me anything, it's cool.'

'And you're OK being around all that?'

'OK, no,' she said. 'Like, I'd prefer not to see it. But honestly you could snort lines of it off my forearm and I don't think I'd feel tempted, no, not at this stage.'

'That's badass,' I said. 'Wow.'

She gave me a little shrug. 'It is what it is.'

'And what was your. You know.'

'Drug of choice?' She shook her head as she took the cup from my hand. 'I don't reminisce about that sort of thing.'

She eased herself back against the counter. I squinted at the percolator. The coffee looked good. It might pull me out of the glue of my own tiredness. But my stomach had holes singed in it. For a long time, I'd thought that I'd discovered a secret to happiness by simply reducing all of my concerns to these questions of velocity, heroin versus coffee versus alcohol versus cocaine versus acid versus weed versus whatever it was that was in the stuff we called MDMA, reducing whatever self I had to streamers of particles shooting through the void and, from there, managing their flow. But it was getting really boring, and also sort of confusing. I rubbed my eyes hard, like I wanted to smush them with my knuckles. I groaned.

'And you do all of this drug free?' I said. 'All of it?'

Helen nodded.

'Wow. That's. Yeah. Man.'

'It was harder to continue than to stop. That's the only reason I stopped.'

'That might take me a while.'

I was holding a cup of coffee that I didn't remember pouring for myself. I watched the bubbles spin and pop. The crema had the rainbow shine of an oilstain. I wanted to tell Helen how I felt as though I'd been sped out of my mother's womb too fast, but how everyone's born prematurely, of course, because who the fuck wants to be here, frankly, when you really look at it, but how I think I'd had an extreme version of that sensation, that I wound up feeling that the womb had never had trustworthy walls, and so neither did the world, and so now I needed to get that feeling of safety to happen whatever way was available. I wanted to tell her about the hole at the end of 'Ithaca' in *Ulysses*, how it was like an underground river sucking everything out of view. I wanted to tell her how the suction of the needle in my wrist made me feel floodwaters in my veins.

'Does it work?' I said.

'Does what?' Helen said.

'Doing all this,' I said, 'without anything to take the edge off.'

'Sort of,' she said.

We were walking from the kitchen back into her room. She unzipped her bag. She hadn't brought much, and all of it looked carefully folded. A smell of fabric softener bloomed out.

'It's more just that the other way doesn't work,' she said. She crouched before a drawer, dropped in a bale of t-shirts. I saw band names: Grinderman, The Strokes.

I was rubbing my upper arms: cold, itchy, both, neither, my nerves couldn't decide. With a yogic smoothness Helen rolled up from where she was hunkering before the drawers, dusted off her hands and said, 'Walk?'

I thought about it for a second, heaved myself up off the office chair I'd let myself fall into, then heard and felt a sigh rise out of me.

'Yeah, go on then,' I said.

*

Somehow it was evening already. The last of the rainclouds had burned off, leaving a brownish, humid sky. We walked towards the sea. Helen told me she had recently split with a boyfriend. They had been together for many years, and had travelled a lot: South America, Southeast Asia, even Antarctica. I asked her about that last one. She told me about the big blue antiemetics-slash-sleeping pills they had to take on the boat from

Punta Arenas to King George Island, because the waves were mountainous, impossible. The force of the ordinary storms was such that they couldn't even walk, she said. They crawled from their berths to the toilet, watched films they'd downloaded to their laptops, stayed deep below decks, feeling the big humming lull of the engines, the bloodnoise of a whale. And then the sudden shock of the light, everything pristine, everything infinite, everything so bright that it hurt, a simplified palette, blue and white, for ever and ever, dropped back through time at the start of the universe, back to the pigments it had all been mixed out of, not that this made sense, of course, she said, because that's not how the universe looked at the beginning, all blurs and bolts and bars and streaks of dirt-coloured light through ashy dark, all that stuff.

'Wouldn't mind one of those big blue pills myself right now,' I said.

'What?'

'The ones you took on the boat. The pills. To stop you getting sick.'

'Oh. Those.'

'Yeah?'

'They weren't blue.'

'Oh.'

'That's something else. That's Viagra.'

'Ah.'

We kept walking. Now and again, Helen put her hand on my shoulder and drew me back, saying, 'You're running.'

'I'm crap at weekends,' I said. 'I've no idea how to slow down.'

Ale-coloured sea-fog was rolling in over the pier. Couples and families and dogs were doing their thing. It should have been nice. It was nice. But I was barely noticing any of it. I had that tight anxiety balled up right there under my ribs. It was stopping me enjoying any of this. I needed something to loosen it up. Every shrilling of every gull, every skirl of car-brakes, every kid's sudden laugh, they seemed to turn into white spikes in the centre of my brain.

A black dog with the long sleek head of a seal was pattering through the sand, kicking up little puffs of sand. Now and then he'd stop and twine in quick lemniscates after his own tail, eyes round and shiny with need.

'Uh,' I said, and tottered.

I'd seen that dog before. He appeared sometimes in my room, once in the mauled yellow foam of a footstool whose ruination would mean a fine from the landlord when I checked out, another time on the chewed wreckage of a wardrobe door that my head didn't remember punching to pieces but which my knuckles certainly did. I blinked and the dog went away the way he did when he was in my room and I opened my eyes again and squinted at an ad that was pasted to one of the lampposts. I'd seen them around before, but I'd never stopped to really look. SERVICIOS EN GENERAL, it read, under a pen drawing of a man with Mr Muscle's body and a face that had a long nose, a big moustache, and a shifty expression. VERY TRUSTWORTHY MEXICAN, the ad continued, in Spanish, I PROMISE. CALL LOMBARDO, and then, in English, PLIS I NEED A YOB. A grainy photograph underneath showed the same man grinning anxiously in full mariachi regalia and foisting the flyer on people who were emerging from the Urquinaona Metro station.

'Do you think that's performance art or a joke or racism?'

Helen squinted.

'Well, you can never really be sure, around here, can you.'

'Around where?'

'Europe.'

'Ah. Yeah. Fair.'

'Thanks for coming out with me.'

'It's no problem. I've been inside for days.'

She squinted at the horizon. Clouds like fiery wool were slowly rolling together into the beginning of a storm.

'And do you know anyone in Mexico?' she asked.

'Just you.'

We'd found our way to a little café near the end of a pier. I remembered being here. I'd wound up lying under a brushy-looking dead acacia, one of the days I'd run out of drugs and couldn't find anyone who had what I wanted. One of the guys who hawk beer cans at tourists had given me a bit of some quartzy-looking shite and I'd snorted it in a public toilet. There'd been a lot of speed in it, a serrated treble jangle mingling with the warm bass feeling I'd wanted, so I'd tried to walk off that spikiness and wound up seven or eight neighbourhoods over. There was a whitish jelly all over my lips from not having drunk water in hours, but the cool of the shade was better than sinking into a pool. Across the way a man with dreadlocks lay on the pavement beside a shuttered newsstand; I noticed that he was one of those who liked wearing a telephone cord as a bracelet. His elbows and back were propped against a pile of sun-beaten magazines. He was talking to a woman in a security guard's uniform who was sitting on an office chair outside a tall apartment building of tinted glass and steel. I laid my hand backwards and curved my fingers to the shape of the gap left where a stone had been dislodged. There was an egg-shaped imprint in the cool, dry dirt. A little crack ran through the smoothness, like the sagittal suture of my own skull. The thoughts had been so hot in my head. Now and then the woman and the telephone-cord guy had shot me worried looks so I'd begun to walk again.

Now, Helen and I had got a table near a family of four, quietly working through plates of chips. The two boys – blond, fourish, sixish – looked over at us, then looked away.

'I know someone who's opened an English school,' Helen said, checking the menu. 'Mexico City. He's not a total basket-case. So. I can send an email.'

'Huh,' I said.

'It's in a beautiful neighbourhood,' she said. 'Lots of plants.'

'I saw these pictures once,' I said. 'In one of these old encyclopaedias that my grandad had. It was just this load of men and women climbing up immense branches through a canopy of big green leaves. And there were Spanish people riding on top of the branches, pushing down with lances. But the leaves were shielding some of the men and women below. And there was this huge sky of pure light, a big yellow nowhere. And people on a cliff, pointing towards the sun.'

'Oh, I know that one,' she said. 'Rivera. Yeah. It's in Cuernavaca. In Cortés's old house.'

'A basic reference, I assume. This is silly.'

'No, no, it's really good. Everybody likes those murals. Because they're really good.'

I drank my Valpolicella, felt the light cherry assault of it dapple my palate, looked at the sea. The waiter brought the bill, an apologetic look on his face.

'We're changing shifts,' he said. 'I've to wrap up.'

'Yeah, that's alright,' I said, and slid my card out of my wallet.

'Thanks. Let me get the terminal.'

He slipped off again, back towards the restaurant.

The raised digits of my card were stuck all over with heroin. I wet my finger, dabbed it up, flipped the card over, found more embedded in the backs of the numbers, then swabbed my gums with the loaded finger. I sat back, took a swig of wine, let the loosening feeling spread through me. A last ripple of blue was visible in the air. It was my favourite colour, that faded, washed-out cyan. I knew that colour from sitting at the back of English class, my homework done, staring dazed out at the cool rinsed blue of the air above the Black Abbey, behind my school. The hull of a rising plane glinted down at me, from the top of a cotton-thick vapour trail; it was the ripper my mother would use to cut across the seams of my school pants when she was fixing the cuffs. That colour went a long way back in my head, to that moment with the encyclopaedias in my grandad's house. There was more to it than the colours, but I didn't want to tell Helen the rest.

I don't remember where everybody was on the evening that I found the books, but I can guess: my grandfather upstairs asleep, my father hacking away at the bush of yellow roses in the garden, my mother stretched out on the sun-chair, swaying herself back and forth with her toe, trying to focus on the book open in front of her. I'd grown bored with being the only one who had to stay inside, in this tank of headachy light, copying out pages from the sixth-class reader, making the loops of the cursive 'T' tap the upper blue line, helping the swoops of the 'y' go down far, but not too far, so they didn't tangle into the letters on the next line, even if those letters didn't exist yet. I couldn't get a single one of them to look alike, and I hated the typed letters for being so regular and well-behaved.

The rooms had that shut-in, rice-papery smell. The light was weighty, pollen-coloured, the way air pollution looks to me now. I pushed the book off the table. It slid further than I wanted it to, onto the floor with a clatter. I could see the blisters on the surface of the table. I didn't know what caused that: craters, or the holes my mother said would stay in your skin if you popped spots. I got up to retrieve the book, hunkering to the carpet, but I couldn't find the energy in my body to lift it up again. I can see myself clearly as I was on that evening: skinny, nine, my knees up past my shoulders, my face cupped in my hands, a little gargoyle. My eyes moved over the cords in the carpet, over the chintzy nap

137

and tassels of the couches and armchairs, their springs pummelled by years of arses until they basically swallowed me to the pelvis when I sat into them, and then over the walls, the dust's polleny turnings in the lit air, catching in a fine grain on a navy cloth heart hung on the wall, stuck through with seven tin swords, a framed *Sgt. Pepper* sleeve with its faded morning blue, photos of the uncles whose names I wasn't allowed to mention in front of anybody, a stained-glass window whose green and red and purple plates framed George Best pumping the air with both fists, and a pencil sketch by my mother of Oliver Plunkett, his flowing hair and thin beard making him look a bit like a girl but also somehow more like a man than either my father or grandfather looked, even though they were bigger than him.

All of it saddened me. I felt too young to be near so many old things. I looked over at the bookshelf by the TV, saw a row of encyclopaedias with frayed cloth covers, the little lattices of the weave showing through, but enough of the blue still lingered for me to recall that peaceful blue of the *Sgt. Pepper* sleeve, as if it had dripped into these books somehow. I pulled one out, felt a book knock my fingers, saw a paperback whose black cover showed a goat's skull wearing reins on it, tea-dark patches showing through the seams and the torn corners. My mother had told me never to touch that one: it had belonged to my uncle, the one I hadn't seen since he'd explained the word *jubilant* to me one day, his voice so deep and tarry, the heart of a tree speaking. I pushed it back into the gap left by the encyclopaedia I'd pulled out. I tidied my books and left them on the table.

The corners of the encyclopaedia had softened, and the cloth was fraying. Inside, the photos were old, but they weren't sad, somehow: there was something young about them, maybe it was just the faded colour palette, the way this made everything hit like morning, from the photos of Abu Simbel and the Sphinx – faded aqua air, golden sand – to pictures of the world's first laser, from Shinto masks to the Swedish galleon hauled up clad in barnacles from where it had sunk off the coast of Stockholm.

My mother and father were talking at the same time when they came in. They were loud, but didn't sound angry. When I looked up my father threw a packet of crisps at me. I checked the label on the crisps to see if they had the inked sprig of a leaf that meant they were vegetarian. My father sat into the armchair behind where I was on the floor so I could lean back against his shins, jouncing his feet rhythmically against the small of my back.

'What have you got there?' my mother said. She was yawning a little.

I held up the book cover for her.

'Oh, wow,' she said. 'I wonder if anyone's opened that since the seventies.'

My father turned on the TV. A song blared out, an urgent, clanging guitar and a woman's breathy voice.

'God,' my mother said. Pollen-yellow light filtered down over her. Ice clinked in her wine glass. 'You remember that one?'

'I do, yeah,' my da said. 'There was a World Cup match on that night.' Then, scratching his eyebrow, watching the screen. 'Blondie, isn't it,' he said.

My mother sucked in and huffed out a long breath. 'Hop the ball, won't you, once in a way.'

My father frowned. Another ad started. Trumpets whined, drums clattered, and I could nearly smell the frying at the restaurants on the screen, nearly smell the cordite sting of the flares. My body ached for elsewhere. Now a train was blurring at high speed past hospitals and graveyards and fountains and hillsides, heading towards the great spaceship glitter of a stadium where everyone was howling, alive, eyes huge and giddy, the eyes of horses that have realised at one and the same time both that they must bolt and cannot bolt. It felt too much. I looked down at the book, turned the page. The humid blue of the sky on the screen was here, too. I ran my finger over the pale blue, over the oil-shine of the word MEXICO printed in bold across the image, a label for the source of that huge, delirious colour and feeling rippling through me. Every molecule was in ebullition, atoms zipping through nowhere, same as in the diagram of the photos that go into a laser that I'd seen. There was a leaf-cool to the greens on the page. It calmed me. The pictures felt as seethingly alive as the pictures that made the advertisement feeling, but in a slower way. Cars were parked under powder-blue air outside a theatre with a mural above the doors, showing a space of smoke and fumes and scarlet drapes. At the centre of that image, an opera mask decorated with a sun and moon hung by a woman's red-nailed fingers over flames where revolutionaries and emperors and Aztec duchesses twisted like dancers. A sleepy Devil half dozed in the corner on a couch, his legs crossed, smiling with pity at the whole spectacle. A smoky feeling climbed up into me from the picture: the feel of what the breathy-voiced woman and that clanging guitar had been singing about, the words *tonight* and *magnificent* climbing into the air in time with the rising of the camera and the rising of the feeling under my sternum. I turned the page, saw the words MEXICO CITY in a caption under a skyline of glassy towers that appeared to be moving towards me through steam. Inset photos showed a man chopping at bananas and smiling as he worked, with another showing a huge truck gouging through the dirt to build a vast tunnel whose cool and echo I could nearly feel sucking me towards it.

Then the ads ended, the speakers changed to the noise of crowds, and I heard a referee's whistle, while my mother uncrossed her legs, crossed them again on the other side, and said, 'Here we go – another hour and a half I won't get back,' while my father huffed out another heavy breath.

'What?' my mother said.

'I didn't say anything.' My father's voice was tired. He watched them kick off, but I could tell he wasn't able to really watch. It was England against Argentina. I had on the bootleg MICHAEL OWEN 10 Liverpool jersey they had gotten me on holiday. My father wanted Beckham to lose because he'd started acting the eejit instead of just playing the game, but he didn't go on about it, not the way the United fans in my primary school went on about Liverpool being shit – that was the word they used, *shit*, that grey-black dragmark sound of a word, like a metal thing scraping on concrete. The TV was on really loud. My mother was rotating a finger and thumb against her temples.

'I'd love that to be me,' I said, watching Michael Owen receive the ball on the far left and sprint towards the box.

'Yes, well, that won't be happening,' my mother said, in a voice that made me think of a stapler pressing down, just that clipped, final sound, leaving holes that never went away. A football had slapped me in the belly and knocked all the air out of me. The picture on the screen didn't go blurry, but I wasn't able to look at it properly now: it was an image of embarrassment. I was too stunned to make any noise. I'd known it was true. Who didn't? But I still wanted to pretend. That's what the TV was for.

'Ah, come on, now,' my da said.

'It won't happen,' she said, more softly this time. She took her hand away from her head and rested her temple against the corner of the armchair. 'You'd have to be making waves by now if you were going to get that far.'

I could feel my mouth, all shivery, a rubber band tug-tug-tugging. It's not that I wanted to cry, I just didn't have a choice, my chest hurt and my mouth was just doing that, as if there was something wobbling and pulling it down at the corners. My da shook his head.

'Tell me I'm wrong,' she said to him, then turned towards me. Her eyes seemed to move over me coldly, watching the hurt spread through my face. I don't know if she knew what she was saying. I wonder if she wasn't just trying to protect me from my own expectations, with the urgency of someone who'd seen other people's expectations get out of control, lead them into worse hurts than they could handle. Either way, the shock and the sting were all that delayed the sobs. 'Anyway, you don't want to be around those people.' She flapped a hand, and I felt as though that hand-flap was her swatting away those people, on my side again. 'Footballers. Successful people. They're all arseholes. Every single one.'

She closed her eyes and rested her head on her hand, her elbow propped on the armrest. 'They're psychopaths. Denis Irwin. Roy Keane. Fucking psychopaths. Why would you want to be a psychopath. They're just what happens when the people who pick on you in school get big and get paid too much.'

My da huffed in and out again and said, 'OK, love. OK.'

David Beckham had just kicked Simeone in the back of the calf and my da was shaking his head, saying, 'I don't even know why I'm surprised.' The crying feeling had gone now. I looked back towards the powdery light drifting through the windows, blurring with the old-photo yellow and the thought of that quarry at the back of our house. I dropped my head, let the last of the pain beat itself quiet inside me, looked down through the encyclopaedia pictures, right into Mexico, diving into the colours before me: a humid river-smell of underground rock rising from the pictures of the statues, the stun of light cutting in from above and cleaning my head empty, that faded morning blue over the dancing shapes of Diego Rivera's Teatro de los Insurgentes mural, sun winking on banana-farmers' machetes like the picture was made of metal rather than ink on paper. That green, that blue: those colours had already become an escape.

*

I heard Helen's feet crunch back across the gravel. The waiter was on his way back with the terminal.

'If you pay for this you're in trouble,' Helen said, lunging for her handbag.

'C'mon, you only had a water. Don't be silly.' I slid the card into the terminal, tapped in my PIN.

'Well, you have no choice, then,' Helen said, tapping on her phone.

'What?'

'I'm emailing that friend with the school,' she said. 'Get you back for the water.'

'It wasn't even a San Pellegrino. Or what's that other one.' I clicked a finger.

'Vichy Catalan,' she said, then added, 'Too late. Sent,' and locked her phone and dropped it into her bag.

'Thanks,' I said to the waiter as he tore off the receipt and handed it to me. 'Shall we, so?' I said to Helen. 'More walking?'

'But no more running.'

'Only figuratively,' I said, then pocketed my wallet and followed her out of the garden of the bar, towards the lights that were switching on one by one along the curve of the waterfront. I saw an unlit pier jutting out into the sea, a black rectangle surrounded by the sea's bigger blackness. Then its lights came on, too, white globes pulsing into the dark, and we kept on walking.

It started off pretty well in Mexico City. Helen had put me in contact with her non-insane friend at the language school, and my Skype interview had been so easy that I'd thought it was a hoax. They offered me the job at the end of the call, started on the visa process, helped me work out flights and passed on the address of a place where teachers pitched up for a couple of weeks until they found an apartment of their own.

My first morning was cold, dripping with rain, and sleepy, as if the whole city was feeling hungover. I had drunk Argentine Malbec on the plane from Montevideo to Santiago and then Chilean Malbec all evening long waiting for the transfer in Santiago and then Mexican Malbec all night long on the plane to Mexico City. But my headache and the syrupy exhaustion had melted away as I got into the taxi. The green of the trees was hypersaturated, heavy on the skin of my right forearm that I left to twist and bob on the draught through the window. Passing every sodden park, I could feel how the city really did once stand on the lake, just this tingle in the air, a fog-cool, as though all the waters of Texcoco before the Spanish had drained it out still hovered suspended in the air, defeating all time. That floaty peace isn't so hard to get back to, I thought.

Leaving the airport, flying up and over and down the big curves of the peripheral highway, the taxi dived through a few tunnels, then slowed along Insurgentes, and the driver flipped the indicator right, and turned, and I looked up and I said, 'Are you fucking serious?' to myself under my breath because there it was: the smoky purples and wild pinks, the uplifted opera mask, the tapering red-nailed fingers, the sleepy Devil and his pitying smile, electricity sparkles spilling through space, tumbling into my veins. It was the mural I'd seen in the book when I was a child. I couldn't believe it. The map line on the screen from here to my new address was a distance of two blocks. I'd made it. I'd found my way here. I'd found the picture. I had to remember to shut my own mouth. I was home, or near enough.

On the street where the taxi left me, there were plants everywhere, bursting up through the gaps in people's walls: monstera, teléfono, begonias, orchids, bird-of-paradise flowers, banana leaves, alcatraces brimming with rain, an enormous palm swaying there, its trunk as thick as a ship's mast. The pores of the concrete in the pavement were plugged green with algae. Laurel and rubber fig tree branches arched together overhead from either side of the street and gave a cool green tunnel feel to it all – a rain cave, the way I'd make the world feel for myself under the covers when I'd been small. I could hear the grunt of roots, buds creaking as they opened.

I wanted all my days to be that first day, when I dumped my things and drank all day in the dim cave of a taquería, watching the park drip, breathing in plant smell. A Sunday feeling had fallen with the drops plinking from the big dinosaur shapes of the palm and banana trees, and I'd felt a hooded peace draw in over me with the lead hood of clouds coming in over the city. I'd seen a picture rise in my head from another encyclopaedia in my grandad's house, Garibaldi under a plant-climbed terrace, looking out over the corrugations of the waves, safely away from home. I love when the clouds burst. The soul for me could be a kind of lone, private rain, each drop holding a picture, the noise of it a wordless speech I can only get to when all the words blur together and cancel each other out, playing themselves out in cables of clause and sentence and paragraphs and stories and splattering over the floor of my skull and becoming nothing at all. There is no meaning, no speech, just the raindrop sound of words falling – their seethe, their fade.

*

My teaching days were long: first class at 6 a.m., the last at eight or nine in the evening. Getting up was hard, but once I'd had a couple of shower beers or some of whatever bottle I'd left cooling in the cistern, I'd be numb enough to almost feel energised.

My students were executives who were too tired to show up – in mind, almost always; in body, not infrequently – or long-term unemployed people who'd mostly be tapping away on their phones or laptops, firing off CVs, trawling LinkedIn, uttering polite chuckles at my shite jokes to make the pretended listening look a bit more effective. I didn't feel too bad about this. I wasn't so present either and, because of my contract, I'd get my money whether or not the students were there or not, so I didn't care. After the early class, I'd sway on my Starbucks chair, cauled under banana leaves and date palm fronds, sucking down vanilla cream cold brew that I loaded with the contents of a hipflask, my legs tingling from the walk along Reforma, past the statues spining the road, looking like blast debris fallen from the rest of the world: a statue of Tito, a statue of Gandhi, a map of Armenia intended to commemorate the genocide. I was sitting on a balcony looking down on every other else-where, in some kind of capital of exile. Gaggles of out-of-town schoolkids would stream across the pedestrian crossing towards the Museo Nacional de Antropología, dozy, up too early, straggling from the hands of their harried teachers. I'd wait for the cold blue to leak into the air, that frost-taste in it, taking me back to the release of morning break in school, that sort of crackling instant between opening a can of something ice cold and fizzy and the taste of it in your mouth – a sound, I know, that I've only ever properly heard when boosted and over-produced in an advert, intended to suggest a total flood of refreshment, but which, nevertheless, was the precise tenor of that fresh cut to the palate left by sucking in cold air. I felt a million places at once, soul blooming southwards to the ice cliffs of Antarctica, but then also the deep peppery nick of soaked hedges blowing me all the way home, chased on Atlantic winds, Irish Sea air, a microscopic bead of salt caught in the wings of a gull flinging in over our garden back home in Kilkenny.

Managing within that sleepy, still-hovering feel of morning was easy. What never went so well was the hot noon glare, when the hangover really began to rage. The city became one big stone dictionary shouting its words all at once. Afternoons would send me way north into the industrial sector, up around Vallejo and Martín Carranza, horizons dogtoothed with refineries and the sloping roofs of warehouses. I'd slog up there on the Metro or Metrobús, through neighbourhoods whose quake-wrecked churches and pavements rucked up by plane trees looked as fucked as I felt, holding together the plates of my skull with my hands. Sliding off the bus, fat drumming in my cheeks, the chitter of the sparrows seeming to say something but nothing I could decipher, I'd fall straight into the sort of wood-panelled bar that opened at six in the morning and had piss-gutters that I could never tell if you were allowed to use or not. I found my kind there, men and women, carefully lifting that day's first drink like they were rescuing a broken bird who'd slammed into a window, their bafflement burning into clarity, even garrulousness, within the space of a few sips. I'd go into the classes with my head ringing, but with enough beery goodwill to be an encouraging, forgiving teacher. I'm not sure I want to think about how I must have smelled.

Evenings, I'd go trekking home through the ashlight, or killing time in another cantina till the Metro emptied, drink and exhaustion close enough to happiness as made no difference, and then home: baggie, foil, lighter, jacks-roll tube under honeyed light.

Obtaining the stuff was a more vexed proposition than it had been in Barcelona: late-night trips through the market cages out the back of Tacubaya Metro, along a walkway of planks, as far as a grille with a screen of smoky glass behind it. A hand would come out for the money, vanish and return with the bag. No change was given. Looking up was a bad idea: the muzzles of assault rifles would be staring back down at you from the level above. Beyond the shoulders of the lads with the guns were the folded tarps and baled-up blankets and phone-charger cables and teddies in nets and all the rest of what got sold there by day. Thanks to the exchange rate I was able to pay the equivalent of under twenty euros for a habit that would cost me four times that back in Barcelona. This exchange rate included the value put on the life of the person doing the selling here as opposed to over in Europe. Did I think about this? No. I thought about getting back home with the bag, to put on all of the music which had once filled my teenage bones with a buzz that I'd mistaken for hope – U2, The Eagles, Pink Floyd, Rory Gallagher, Neil Young, The Rolling Stones – and which I now, despite still listening to it, find terribly silly and dated, and sink back into the ancient couch whose springs were so pummelled by years of tenants that it made a liquid hug around me. The rhythmic '*Hai!*' of kids doing karate would trickle up to me from the studio downstairs in the same building. In the park, joggers ran laps and dogs scuffled and yapped and I'd watch them and smile. The day was about getting to this place and this place only, the only nowhere available, whatever bundle of memories and anxieties that went by my name scattered to atoms, and my mind the surface of a pool stilling slowly over.

*

Not all the using was solo, just most of it. Socially, it's fair to say that I fell in with a bad crowd, party people with the same surnames as presidents and eighties drug lords. I was oblivious to this at the beginning, but then I brought a journalist friend of mine to the art gallery where we'd have most of our parties and he returned from his round of the room looking concerned.

'That guy over there,' he said, pointing discreetly, his hand around his glass. 'You know what he said to me?'

'Do you want some coke?'

'Well, that, yes, but my asthma, you understand. No. He said he was Carlos Salinas's nephew. He looked pretty rueful about it.'

'Huh.'

'And that guy he's talking to, he's one of the Caro Quintero cousins.'

'That guy? He's a vet.'

'He's more than that,' my friend said. 'You know, I'm not sure about this old party. I feel a bit gamekeeper turned poacher.'

'Consider it research.'

'I'm not an anthropologist.'

I think this must have been the time where I woke up shivering on a couch beside my friend Angela, still in our too-thin party clothes, a din from the caged luxury dogs echoing around us in the room where we'd passed out. The glass table was scored with gritty lines of bluish powder.

'What the fuck,' said Angela, sitting slowly up, making eye contact with a miniature poodle flinging herself in little curly somersaults against the metal bars of the cage.

'Whose house is this?' I said.

'That vet guy's,' she said.

'Oh.' I felt very awake all of a sudden. 'Do you want to get breakfast?'

Angela looked past the dogs and around the room. I followed her gaze with mine, saw a wooden pallet loaded with Nike shoeboxes, all wrapped in plastic.

'I think that'd be a good idea, yeah,' she said.

The key was in the door. We let ourselves out quietly. I wasn't sure what street we were going to step out onto. The sun punched me in the face. When my vision cleared I was looking at a bunch of enormous papier-mâché skulls in bright colours – lime green, pink, toothache orange – interspersed with tall dragons and insects and skeletal birds of the same neon colours, all seeming to move and flow down the pedestrianised spine of the avenue, under eucalyptus trees whose arching shapes made me think of nymphs, or dancers.

'Oh, I know where we are,' Angela said, as she grabbed me by the arm. 'I know a place.'

'Are those all definitely there?' I said, hanging back a little, pointing my cigarette at the animals walking down the middle of the street.

'Sure,' Angela said.

In those days, waking up was a roulette wheel.

I woke up on floors crunchy with broken glass in postcodes that I'd had no idea existed. I woke up on the floor of a cantina moments after passing out, slipping from my chair, moated by my own puke, the noise of the other drinkers' applause echoing around the room. I woke up in courtyards surrounded by plastic tables whose surfaces were covered in sticky rings and toppled those red cups that you see in American high school films. On a holiday to Chiapas I woke up in a cemetery, lying on a grave, deep in unkempt grass, a plastic bottle of pox in my fist, while people walking to Mass at the little yellow church shook their heads at me. Later, after I'd stopped teaching English, while I was on assignment for a newspaper, writing about refugees fleeing violence in Central America, I woke up at the foot of a golf cart on an island in Belize, a six-pack of Guinness and a slice of pizza with some weed crumbled onto it sitting on the driver's seat, 'One of These Nights' by The Eagles was playing on my phone. I woke up in parks, under trees. I woke up in the gardens of some kind of cultural centre, the two suited security guards ushering me across the lawn with the beaming obsequiousness of butlers. I woke up with sand in my pockets on a beach in Acapulco after someone decided it would be cool for us to drive there because we were too high to sleep. I woke up in someone else's beat-up car wearing my swimming trunks and her V-neck sweater, the owner asleep in the back, she and I both soaked, a bare tree looming over the car, its branches fucked by disease, growing in a wild, spherical tangle that I felt convinced for a moment was a nervous system beaming some kind of terrible information at me.

Two tired-looking men in paint-spattered builders' overalls were sitting on the step across from the car, eating sandwiches. They stopped chewing when they saw me whirl around to stare at them through the passenger window. When I checked my reflection in the rearview mirror I startled myself almost as much as I must have startled them. I woke up on the couch of an artist's studio, gasped, sat up, belt jangling, shirt open, groping towards the bathroom, only to walk through the door of a boardroom where a meeting was in session. Sometimes when I woke up I wasn't even sure if I had woken up, and if I wasn't maybe instead sliding down the helix of some kind of after-death hallucination. When I woke up alone in my room I'd groan with relief, pull the shades down, put in earplugs, put on the football – Europa League, Serie A, Brazilian provincial league, even Chelsea if I was really desperate – and feel the slow cool drip of the live-feed connecting me like an umbilical cord with something beyond the burning-meat tang of my own sweat and the tea-dark gloom of my apartment, drinking or huffing or shooting till I was a recalcitrant koi hiding out in the murk at the bottom of a pond.

What woke me most mornings was a sudden crump of pain in my bladder: that's usually how I knew I was coming down. I'd barely make it to the toilet in time, doubled over around the Y-shaped red crease of pain printed into my back and front, either shivering or shaking: I couldn't tell the difference. I was eating so badly that my weight had dropped to around forty-five kilos. Food was medicine, a boring kind, the kind that didn't get you high. I'd microwave a chunk of frozen soy-meat and wolf it down, standing up, often right by the toilet in case I vomited. My gums softened and rotted until they had the mushy pink feel of papaya on the turn. Now I find it hard to imagine what kind of person would have had sex with me in that state, but people did, a lot of them, and I was usually the one who cheated, who told people to fuck off for being too affectionate, blaming my leper feet and their toe-gaps all pocked with needle scabs on bedbugs that my apartment did not have.

*

I remember trying to put together more than two days not high or drunk by going on a silent meditation retreat in the mountains outside Oaxaca. Without drugs or alcohol, the present came at me as an explosion of splinters. Every shred of sensory datum seemed like it was telling me something. I felt compelled to write everything down, but that wasn't allowed on the retreat, so I started to transcribe everything I was looking at in my head, running my mind again and again over the imagined paragraphs. Between sessions I'd stand on the balcony of the dormitory gripping the rail until my knuckles whitened, rocking myself back and forth. The beauty of the place rained down on me unfelt: the brick arches of the walls with grass and nopal cactus sprouting up through the gaps, the figures on bikes shirring past over the dirt tracks, wheels trailing thin manes of dust; the ruck of the Sierra Madre turning blue in the dusk, the bake of the heat going way deep into my bones. When the bell went, I'd exit the chamber in a sulk, go stand in front of the colonnade of maguey cacti, wish I could be them. They were time's most basic signature: slender at the midsection during decades of thirst, edges a rust-stitch of spines, their bases hardened to stone-coloured wood, the freshest portions aiming towards the sun and looking, to me, like the heads of sleeping lizards. That scene in *Rocky* came to me, the one where they razor his eyebrow to release pressure, the commentator shouting, 'He just wants the bell!' I did, too: the bell that ended every session, I'd count down to it one breath at a time.

Within half an hour of getting out of the retreat I was drunk again. The cantina was showing *Breaking Bad*, the episode where Walt strangles Krazy-8 with a bike lock. The barman stared listlessly up at the screen, munching peanuts. Me, I was crying, because the guy being strangled was stabbing away with a long shard from a broken plate, the motion of his arm automatic, cold, robotic, not stopping even when he was choking with a noise like he was gargling ceramic chips. My hand's motion lifting the bottle and the glass to my mouth and putting it back down onto the bar was the same as that of the guy stabbing on the screen. I didn't even want to be drinking. It was just the only thing that even sort of worked to quiet all of the speech in my head. On the TV Krazy-8 coughed and spluttered his last. His hand dropped one last time. The shard fell and shattered. His expression had the blank release of a saint. The barman clicked his tongue, looked away from the screen, then turned to me, saying, 'Another?' If he registered the look on my face, he was discreet about it. I loved him for that. People were so kind. It was all so moving.

'Always,' I said, and slid the empty beer and the empty shot glass towards him, trying to be helpful.

*

I drifted apart fairly quickly from Helen, the friend who'd gotten me the job. She was deep in with her recovery group and an on-and-off thing with this artist guy she'd met. He was forever on and off the spike, too, which took up a lot of her time.

'Codependency again,' she'd joke, without seeming to find it in any way funny.

'It's hard to say "no" to people when they need you,' I'd say, even though I was another one of the people she should probably have started saying 'no' to. She'd trek north from her parents' house way south of the city, bringing me sandwiches made by her mother, or pillows and duvets because I didn't have any. I'd never be where she was expecting to find me. I'd be spilling out of an Acapulco chair or coming down from the night before surrounded by people she didn't really know, insisting she sit there with the duvet baled up between her knees until the pill people I was with got bored of me.

The on-off boyfriend, Diego, and I got on really well. He'd lived in Barcelona when we'd been there, but that hadn't been where they'd met. The three of us would go to her parents' holiday home at Yautepec and silo ourselves off with a shared bag, while she drifted around reading or texting her sponsor. One birthday party got out of control. His friends and mine outnumbered hers, and she withdrew to the garden, stood by the edge of the pool. During a lull where my conscience managed to prick me through all the stuff in my system I walked over to her, said I was sorry.

'It's alright,' she said, squinting at the water, one hand gripping a homemade suero, the other clasping the elbow of the arm holding her drink. 'It's even sort of clarifying.'

'About?'

'About getting away from it.'

She sipped her mix of sparkling water and lemon juice and salt. The pool filter hummed in the silence. From the house came the trancey whump of the psychedelic electrocumbia that her boyfriend was obsessed by. 'I'm not guilt-tripping you,' she said. She blessed the air, a priest at the end of Mass. 'You're an addict. You're absolved.'

I said nothing, just felt the barb sink into my chest.

'It's not so bad in the city,' I said.

She laughed and said, 'You've been here ten minutes. Nobody who likes it here really lives here.' She put a hand through her hair, let it flop down again. Over on the patio Diego was reeling around flirting with two girls, doubled over laughing one second, leaning back to put some momentum behind his own shouting the next.

'Really would rather be nowhere at all than here sometimes,' she said.

'What, dead?'

'Oh, no. Just. Off the grid.'

Her phone flashed in her hand.

'That's my sponsor,' she said. 'You mind if I take this?'

'Oh, no, go ahead,' I said, putting my hands up, backing away, moving towards the lit patio, the noise, the laughs, their weird cold echo in the dark.

That party, talking with Helen by the pool, watching Diego larking about, that might have been our last party together. I'd already quit the English teaching because I found that the stress of teaching was more acute than the stress of travelling around the country pitching stories to media outlets about drug violence in Mexico. I wasn't so interested in the blood and guts, which were relentless. I found that pornographic. I was interested in how it felt to have your life and future milled by interests beyond your control or comprehension: the police, the government, the economy, how the three of them worked together, became something you might as well call a cartel. Insofar as I ever 'got into this', how I got into this was quite simple. I used to write book reviews for a magazine in Ireland. Over time I began to pitch book reviews related to the countries I was living in, because that way I could understand them better, I thought. Once I pitched a review plus a feature about *Midnight in Mexico* by Alfredo Corchado. I emailed him asking if he fancied an interview. He emailed back saying he'd far rather introduce me to the journalists he knew in the city at a cantina one night. I kept going back to that cantina. Contacts, emails, strings began to land in my lap. Bit by bit the money earned from writing outweighed the money earned from teaching. I went all over the country, all over Central America, all over the Caribbean. Not all of the stories appeared, but I was used to that. It was the same with my novels, my poems, my short fiction. Writing wasn't meant to do anything but burn you out. The nugatory quantities earned just made sure that burn was nice and slow rather than all at once. It was a reality that made me think of the meditating demons, the monks poisoning themselves with amber sap, the martyrs in the Inquisition bonfires slowly watching their own shanks blacken and fibre. I didn't want to be a shiny-shoes journalist. I wanted to be a dirty-boots journalist. I felt far closer to the people I met for articles than I did to other people who wrote articles 'about' those people. I wasn't American, I wasn't bougie, I wasn't on a retainer, I hadn't paid for my education. I didn't get how it felt to be that poor, that scared, that desperate, but at least I got that I didn't get it.

Once I went for tacos with a colleague at an overpriced restaurant in La Roma, Mexico City, a neighbourhood utterly destroyed by travel supplements telling English speakers how cool it is there. In between fending off vendors, he told me about how it was to report on the latest caravan to make its way out of Central America and weave its way up through Mexico.

'There were more journalists than migrants, man,' he said, shaking his head. 'You'd go talk to somebody and they'd have this weary look on their face, going, "I told one of you people already." The words come out as a recitation; they were already quotes. Feels really bad.

Because you're not there in a clinical context either, are you? Like, you're re-traumatising people by having them drag over this really incredibly fucking shitty story, right, and then, at the end, all you do is' – he raised a hand, tapped the air: an imaginary notebook – '"Sweet, thanks for the quote! *Bon voyage!*", and off you go.' He shrugged, took a sip from his bottle of sparkling water, and wagged his finger for 'No' as a guy walked up to us trying to hawk a tray of cacti.

A day or so later, at the shelter near the Misterios Metro station in northern Mexico City, I met with some young Honduran women who'd been attacked in their homes for being trans. They hated the city – the heat, the cram, the harassment from men, the exhaustion, those surreal moments where the sky is the colour of the desert, the pollution shimmer a wave of mercury that never quite breaks.

One woman, Melina, told me about a panic attack she had on the Metro. 'Everything's a panic attack all the time. Just that feeling of wanting to get sick but nothing wants to come up. We're below poor, we're below homeless, there's nowhere on the map where we'd be safe,' she said. 'And anyone who talks about anything else but this feeling is a liar. And anybody who can talk about this feeling in a calm way is a liar, too. And anyone who apologises for not getting it is a liar, too, because to me they're bragging, thinking they've done enough by listening. They don't understand this tiredness. They don't even understand that they don't understand. But what I know doesn't feel worth know-ing, either, it's just more and more tiredness building up on you, a heavy black lagging of powder. I look at old history pictures and I see the same feeling. Or I hear things from the Bible, about crossing the desert and all, and I get that feeling. This feeling of everything being too heavy, and everywhere being too far away. My body feels too heavy to carry around sometimes. I'm not alive and I'm not dead. I can't tell you what I am. On the Metro yesterday I felt sure that I was able to see everyone's heart through their ribs. I felt sick. I saw my heart moving in rhythm with theirs – squeezing, opening, squeezing, opening. To see the veins, the blue, the red, the lumpy shape moving under all of our skins, and the sound, the drumming sound, the squelch, it made me want to stop. I didn't want to carry this body around anymore. But I still got off at my station and I walked back here. Because whether I like it or not, my body is going to keep moving until I stop or something stops me. And it doesn't matter how tired I am. It's not my choice. I keep going, stubborn, you know, stubborn past wanting to be here, just being here, whatever.'

*

Around this time, I was not what you'd call fairly seasoned, but I was harder to faze. I'd been pulled aside by police and had guns pointed at me by people who were maybe police but also maybe not. I'd gone out looking for the bodies of the forty-three disappeared Ayotzinapa students, following a deer hunter as he sank a metal pole into loose-looking ground to see if a blackish seepage or a foul smell oozed up, indicating the presence

163

of a cadaver. I'd seen the blackened zeroes and tattered clothes that marked places where people were burned alive. I'd seen the blood pools, the goremarks, the particular bubbled look of the stain you get on a floor where someone's been forced to drink Clorox, then taped to a chair to die. I don't remember how drunk or high I was at these moments: but I sense it was probably not very, because whatever or how much I'd consumed, the tart sting of the air in those places would sober up anyone – that chlorinated cut, high in the nose, the smell of fear itself, the smell of life, the smell of life reduced to its purest element: fear.

So, the idea of going to a protest with Helen about the disappeared trainee teachers was not frightening to me. I'd seen videos of Molotov cocktails bursting into flaming manes against the door of the Presidential Palace, and I wanted to see it again. Why the disappearance of the students rather than any other proved to be the moment so many people snapped feels impossible to account for. Nobody I've talked to can, either. We have our guesses: how this police violence against teachers accompanied a wave of reforms intended to wash away the pillars of Mexico's post-revolutionary education system; how the police had been caught doing unimaginable stuff that previously only the cartels had been caught doing. I'd seen clips: people fleeing gunshots, the ragged huffing of panic on the mic, blood and glass and red police lights, the students lined up with bruised faces in the corridor of what was clearly an army barracks. Some of the missing students had mothers who'd fought alongside Lucio Cabañas in the Dirty War of the

1970s, when the Mexican state had flown paratroopers into the Tierra Caliente to terrorise pockets of Marxist rebels and their families. Weeks after their disappearance, you'd go into a fruit shop and see the faces of all forty-three missing young men staring out from posters pasted to the back wall. People were about to blow. There was no way I was going to skip the protest. We'd set off from the memorial of the Tlatelolco massacre, on that big square, the Plaza de las Tres Culturas, under the modernist housing units, beside the wrecked church and near the plaque that commemorates the battle that saw the Emperor Cuauhtémoc captured by the Spanish and the end of the resistance. *Neither victory nor defeat*, the plaque reads, *but the birth of the pueblo mestizo that is the Mexico of today.* For what seemed hours groups from the Politécnico and the Universidad Nacional Autónoma de México trickled in, carrying flags. Back in '68, when the troops had opened fire on this square, it had been their counterparts who'd died, or fled into the huge housing units, or found other ways to escape. When you read reports from people who were there, they talk about how first ambulances turned up to collect the bodies, and then army trucks, and then garbage trucks.

Ayotzinapa and Tlatelolco blended in the air, and the sky was low and rainy, a ceiling with rotten plasterwork. Heading south through a highway tunnel, the hollers and the chants turned to river noise, turned the seethe of fear in my veins into exhilaration. It was a better lostness to getting wasted, vanishing into that ocean sensation of everyone around, but washing me towards something, all the way to the blood-coloured stone of the Palacio Nacional and the massed ranks of cops behind their shields. Rioters in black bloc made shit of the place – the fronts of banks, Starbucks, bars dashed to pieces, like an avalanche had hit. Livid scars of graffiti were all over the black metal statues of statesmen and soldiers. I felt a pulse of euphoria high in my chest.

That, though, is more or less where the good vibes ended. A friend got a jet of tear gas right in the face because she was putting a bouquet into one of the vents in the metal walls they'd put up around the Palacio. That thinned our group: a couple of people went home with her. Those who stayed inched back from the front, joined in the chants, kept looking over our shoulders. The day darkened. It started to drizzle. I'm not sure when Helen and I became separated in the crowd, but there was a tidal motion to it, a heave back and forth. She'd been at all the big marches after the disputed election of 2006, so her instinct was to fall back: she got it. My instinct was to push forwards. The Saturday before, protesters had managed to scorch the door of the Palacio Nacional. But today the riot cops stood there yawning and texting behind their shields until the crowd chanted itself hoarse, and then they cleared the space, without even looking as though they were trying. They chased us down a corridor of waiting cops, ushered us into a long bus. We were a morass of limbs, a stopped rush-hour Metro. The humid press of other people, the shouts, the cries, the terror, the lads filming what was happening, the fact that they could do this and none of it would matter, it all made my chest tighten so hard and so fast that my mind flowed up out of the top of my head, yellowly translucent goopstrings sucked flush to the ceiling of the bus. What was happening to Helen? Cops always treated women worse, especially if they stood up for themselves. As for myself, I'd already broken the law just by being at the protest without a media pass. I was a foreigner, they could deport you for intervening in national politics, and the government was taking a very broad interpretation of that: a couple of Chilean musicians had been picked up in a sweep after one of the mass marches a few weeks before. They'd been busking, apparently. Whatever they'd been doing, they were put on the first plane back home. That was about to be me, I thought.

The door clattered open. It was impossible to tell how long we'd been driving for. Hard light and cool air flooded the bus. I heard gasps and curses: we were all too tired to do much more. I saw a big precinct, a lot full of smashed cars, the bloody neons of a by-the-hour motel, some women leaning against the sill, not so much curious to see what was happening as mildly intrigued to have something else to stare at while they waited.

'Come on,' said a cop by the door, flicking his hand towards the building. 'Come on, come on.' It was like he was directing cattle. People followed his instructions, rubbing the backs of their necks, rotating their shoulders. The bus emptied. I lingered. The cop poked his head in, saw me and shook his head, laughing. 'Jesus Christ. You fucking idiot. Just get the fuck home, will you?'

I went to follow the stream of people going up the steps and through the doors, along another gauntlet of cops.

'Not there,' the cop by the door said, grabbing me by the shoulder and shoving me in the opposite direction. 'There.' He pointed towards the security fence, where the barrier was up. 'There. Go home. I told you.'

One or two people in the line going through the door turned and shook their heads. One clicked his tongue and looked away.

'So, you're throwing back the white ones?' I heard a woman say to a cop as she passed. He laughed. Then she was through the door, too.

I got out of the gate and staggered into the avenue. The sudden grind and squall of the traffic stopped the air going in and out of my lungs. I pasted myself against the fence. My heart was going ninety. I was way, way south, beyond Taxqueña, and I'd done that thing they said you should do at protests, where you don't bring your bank cards and only a bit of cash. I'd have to walk home. I squinted at the road signs, felt a fatigue spread a desert through my body, with a hard wind blowing through it. The shock was ebbing now, bringing the cold instead. I zipped up my jacket and started to walk, my body wobbling with the draught of every car that raked past.

For the first part of the walk, I was sustained by the idea that once I got to Insurgentes, my familiarity with that strip of chain restaurants and bars might somehow convert the ground under my feet into a kind of conveyor belt that would bear me smoothly home. This did not happen. I was so out of it with thirst, hunger and the beginnings of withdrawal that at every pedestrian crossing I got honked or jostled. Every road felt as impassable as a river. At one point I tripped chasing a hundred-peso note that turned out to be a flyer for a micro-loans company. My foot caught on an uneven bit of pavement and I went over, mouth-first into the ground, knocking a triangular chunk out of one of my front teeth. I hauled myself up, started walking again, but quickly understood it would be impossible to go any further. I let myself flop onto the ground, lay spread-eagled on my back. Late-shift workers were hurrying out of the mall, or hailing buses, or jogging for the last Metro. Too many of them were stopping to look at me. I heaved myself upright, my mouth parched, my body heavy, my head whumping like someone was playing a bass-drum pedal inside the front of my skull, my jeans torn and bloody, my shirt sweat-stained under the arms, my face greasy, forced myself to walk again. At last, I let myself fall against the whitewashed pillar by the entry to an all-night open-air parking garage. A kid a bit younger than me was sitting in an office chair in the kiosk. He wheeled it back, craned his head out, said, 'You need money or something?'

'Just water,' I said. 'Maybe a sit.'

His foot tapped. He jingled change in his pocket.

'What happened, bro?'

'Was at that protest, wasn't I.'

He sucked his teeth and said, 'No mames.' His thumbs were in his belt loops. 'That got heavy.'

'It got heavy.'

'Yeah, OK,' he said, and jerked his head towards a shed that had a mattress on the floor, covered with a rug like one of my ma's old Foxford ones that she kept in the boot of her car.

'Where'll you sleep, though?' I said, following him through.

'Oh, I won't,' he said. 'I'm on till seven. You might have to nip out then. Guy on dayshift has a pit bull.'

'Shit.'

'No, no: it's just too friendly, the dog. Big slobbery baby. You won't get a wink.'

'You know what address this is?' I said.

The kid gave it to me. I felt my stomach sink. I was miles away. If I put some distance behind me while it was still cold the next morning, then maybe I could do it. I was gearing up for a trek through the desert. I hated myself for drawing the comparison: I'd interviewed people who'd been kidnapped, taken to the US border, sent across with backpacks full of fentanyl and only a tin of tuna to get them through the journey. I knew this wasn't that, and yet there was my ego projecting the self-aggrandising analogy for me, same as those bougie cunts that I hated.

'Also,' the kid said, and went out for a second, returning with a bottle of Peñafiel and some biscuits with jam in them. I nearly wept, but instead I just held up my phone and asked him if he had a charger.

'iPhone?' he said.

'Oh, God, no.'

He held up his and said, 'Use mine?'

'Don't know anyone's number by heart,' I said.

'Don't worry about it,' he said, a brightness in his voice that I couldn't tell if it was fake or not. 'You'll feel better with a nap behind you.'

Sleep didn't come quickly. I kept jolting awake just as I was about to drop off, sure that I was still walking through the dark. When I did finally go under, my dreams were of crammed cells, scratchy stone floors, people banging on bars and hammering their fists against plexiglass. When the kid opened the door later in the night he was holding a Styrofoam cup of atole and half a cake bar held inside a twist of plastic packaging. My mouth felt like a cave full of cobwebs and my head was a tight sphere of pain, but I felt bad at how nice he'd been, so I kicked back the rug and said, 'I'll be off, honestly, you get in there for a rest. Before the dog turns up.'

'That fucking dog, man,' he said through a groan-yawn, holding out the cup and the cake bar as he sat down on the blanket

I did OK for a while, munching and sipping in alternation as I walked north, sugar-rush quickening me ahead of the pain-thud in my skull, but, as the morning began to heat up, and the pedestrians got more harried and numerous, and the traffic thickened on the avenue, with its skirl of brakes and din of horns, I couldn't take it anymore. I slid down an alley, kept walking, looking for somewhere to lie down and shiver until the various crashes had passed off. I found myself in the back of a market and lay down on a tarp. It was well past seven in the morning: if the place was going to open today, it'd have opened by now, so I figured nobody would bother me.

When I woke up this time, it was to a yellow glare over an empty square, the crash of distant car-noise. I lay there on one elbow and yawned and watched the other people who'd washed up here: a guy with a towel belted around his head standing sobbing at a palm tree in the corner; a woman with short hair and two missing eye-teeth and an Axl Rose bandana who was carrying a carton of cigarettes and chewing gum. When the lights went red, she'd move between the cars. When they went green, she'd sprint back to the square and go back to scratching furiously at herself. The people passing through passed through fast, skirting the edges, eyes to the ground. There was a hoarding above the square, an ad for some church or other, the words PARE DE SUFRIR written in violet letters above a blazing fire.

I watched a father and son working away at a torta truck, hammering breaded milanesa flat with the butt of a Coke bottle. The son whisked up an omelette, laid it out with a rich spatter on the hotplate. The smell had my stomach growing fangs and nipping at my gizzard. I watched him build the sandwiches layer by layer, bolillo scooped empty, then a layer of mayo, a layer of refried beans, then sliced avocado, tomato, lettuce, the top of the bolillo roll. I'd have eaten the wad of dough he threw balled-up into the bin. The stall was stuck all over with clippings of the father and son in the ring, the son on his knees in yellow starbursts of indigo spandex over his chest and shoulders, on his knees in front of San Judas and Santa Muerte statues, his father watching with his arms folded and a towel over his shoulders. Eventually my stomach got tired of yowling at me. I tuned out, watched the luchador masks decking the space above the vitrine as they swayed in the wind: El Santo and Blue Demon and Mil Mascaras, the spiked tricolour cowl, futuristic gold spikes of Abismo Negro, the fly-eye textures of Tinieblas. I saw the father's broken-flat nose, bottle-scar marks on his forearms from what must have been a ring-pole. Across the road a guy on paint-thinner swayed back and forth, picking his lip, grinning at his reflection. The lights went red and a skinny topless guy around my age ran in front of the cars, rolled out a cloth tarp loaded with broken glass, dived again and again on it until his chest and back ran with blood. Then the lights changed, and he stood, rolled up his mat and went with his hand out to the cars to see who had their windows down, who might give him change.

It was nearly a relief to accept the level meant for me at all along.

I was hungry, but stuff rots so fast in the heat that going through the bins didn't seem worth it. I wasn't sure anybody else around here had the stomach for it, either, to judge by all the turds all over the dark corner of the square. The main thing was getting water. Hunger I could wait out: matter of fact, I leaned into the hunger, knowing that the floatier I got from my empty stomach, the harder whatever dose I managed to cadge would hit me. I was too tired to move, and too hungry. Eventually the hunger would hurt too much to sleep through, and I'd have to move. Until then, though, I dozed some more, my dreams a jigsaw puzzle flung in the air.

The worst of it was that the square was around the corner from the house of a woman I used to go out with. I loved her house. I loved looking down from the mellow glow of the living room over the streets, able to pretend for a second that I was one of those people who lived such a calm life. The old Porfiriato houses were painted in cake tones – deep marzipan pink, piped-sugar orange, lime-cream green. Even the browns were deep and rich enough to make you want to sink your teeth into it. If I arrived in the neighbourhood before our dates, I'd sit at a Krispy Kreme beside the hospital, look up at a house where the brownish light inside its corner sitting room was a photograph from a time when people had time to read all the books on their shelves. A replica of the Tlaloc outside the Museo de Antropología stood by the window. Before the light went out of the sky, that statue looked photographed, too, from one of those archaeology magazines whose images all seemed to have been taken early one spring morning in the late sixties. Munching my doughnuts, worrying my tongue deep into the cajeta centres, I'd almost be able to inhale the life of that room: the dry-rice odour of paper, the brand of fabric softener used by the people living there, the taste of its dust. When it was time to go back home, I'd enter into the cram of the Metro, try to sleep off the wish to live somewhere else, but never manage to. Now I couldn't do any of those things. Now I was afraid of being seen by her. I couldn't go to her door and ask her to take me in because it hadn't been that kind of arrangement.

By late afternoon, when the brassy colour of the sky had begun to dull and the stink of the bins had begun to deepen and ferment, my mouth was too sticky to sleep through. I walked up to the torta stand and asked for a Dixie cup of agua de limón from the kinder looking of the two guys working there, then pretended I couldn't find any change while the guy waved my gestures away and said,

'Whatever, man, it's five pesos.' I had become everybody I'd ever refused change to, everybody I'd looked through, everybody I'd shaken my head at and said, 'Sorry, another time' to on those days when I was in a good enough mood to be polite. I hovered around the edge of a little wooded square where there was a Tierra Garat café. The terrace was packed. My body tingled all over with anticipatory shame. I'd never done this. I'd never had to. In my head I workshopped and tossed away possible lines the way I'd used to do with my paragraphs back in the times when I'd been able to write what I thought of as literature, what others might have at least considered as literature, if only to reject it. The workshopping didn't work. I didn't know how I was going to start begging. I could try a hard-luck story about being mugged. I could tell the truth, but the truth took ages, and people with long sob stories annoyed me. Then again, they annoyed me so much that I reached quickly and briskly for my wallet and gave them more than I might have if I weren't trying to make up for my own irritability, but I also felt too guilty at potentially discommoding someone for that long that I wasn't sure if I should even try. You look enough like people's worst fears for themselves I guess they'll try to ward off that fear by giving you what you need, I decided. It's what I always meant by giving, anyway.

I was about to make my move when a man in his fifties with dyed chestnut hair sneaked in ahead of me, unzipped a guitar case, and started bashing out a cover version of 'Sweet Caroline'. I couldn't double up on him: he was working, I'd just be begging. So, I sat through 'Love Me Do' and a Supertramp song, watched him go table to table with his hand out, and I wondered how much longer I'd need to wait until there were enough new customers to get something out of them. I was sitting under an alcove with a Virgin Mary statue in it, dead roses in a disposable coffee cup at her feet. My eyes scanned the terrace. I felt someone's gaze on me, turned, looked, saw a woman waving me over to her table. As I approached, I apologised in Spanish, started to talk about losing my wallet. She looked at me, her gaze totally steady, and said, 'I can give you a thousand pesos, but I don't think this is all what you need.' Her accent wasn't local. A barista watched me from the doorway, giving me the same look of threat and disgust as everyone I'd bumped into the day before, and in the morning, too. The woman pointed at me and looked to the barista, then switched to Spanish, saying, 'Get him one more of these' – she shook her cup at him – 'and one of those cheesecakes, yes?' She was wearing a leopard-print hoodie complete with little roundy ears. I felt annoyed with her for a second. I'd have preferred her to just offer me money. In a choice between hunger and the dose, you pick the dose because first it numbs hunger and then it makes you too tired to feel hungry once it's gone.

'This man bothering you?' the barista said. 'Want me to help?'

'Help get him his order.' She dismissed the barista with a wave of her hand. Then she looked at me. 'So, will you sit or what?' When I did, she pushed a packet of Marlboro Red towards me.

'So,' she said. 'Rough day?'

I didn't know what to say. She seemed to be speaking to me from the middle of a tunnel of white headrush needles.

'And water, too,' she said, when the barista reappeared with the cake and the coffee.

My hand tremored too strong for me to open the sugar.

'Here.' Her nails were claws, diamanté-rimmed crimson, with a lemniscate braid of silver going up the middle. She made short work of the sachets. 'You need a lot of sugar, no? The comedown. The heroin, no?'

I said nothing.

'In my country,' she said, 'I flipped two cars on heroin. Driving. I killed two people.' Two of the claws were held up in a 'V' towards me. 'And this on two separate occasions. One before the recovery, another in the relapse.' She said it re*lápse*. I liked that.

I had forked up a bit of cheesecake too soon. The gluey paste of it stuck to the roof of my mouth.

'I was in ICU then,' she said. 'Nobody was happy when I woke up. This is not self-pity, this is fact. Six years and three countries ago.'

I looked at the level of coffee in her cup. She'd be gone in a few minutes. Then the barista'd chase me away. I took a bigger bite of the cake, took a big gulp of the coffee. I already felt full but I kept cramming it down. I wanted to get back to my building before it was dark. I needed all the energy I could get.

She kept talking.

'Now I work as perfumier here. Candles, air fresheners, personal fragrances, all that. I thought I had lost this. It all comes back. It can come back so much faster than you think.'

'How's that meant to happen?' I said.

She gave a one-shoulder shrug.

'You come to a meeting, I think.' She checked her watch. It was chunky and gold. 'One starts in some minutes. You can come with me.'

'I'm worried about my friend,' I said. 'I want to check in on her but she has my phone.'

The woman – her name, she told me, was Noura – slid her phone across the table.

'I don't even know my own,' I said.

'She has family here?'

'Oh, loads. A fucking army, man. And she's in some recovery programme or other, too. So, she's one of yours.'

'So, you won't be the only one looking for her.' She shrugged. 'If something bad was going to happen, it would have happened by now. So just turn it over.'

She got her phone out, checked the screen.

'There's no obligation. But if you can hang in with us for an hour, I can take you wherever you need to be then. Worst case, you waste an hour to get a ride home, then forget it ever happened.' She sucked on her cigarette, spat smoke, shrugged. The tic felt cheesy to me, a take-off of the stoicism you see in films or whatever: which maybe was her intent, I don't know. But thinking, now – of the way my prose has a kind of baked, ceramic hardness, a theatrical mask, and how my mannerisms are fixed, too, anticipations more than responses, my brain quickly going, 'OK, this situation is the same as that situation, so contain it the same way,' that kind of stuff – and I wonder what other mode is left when you've been outside any other kind of framework for being around people other than the one you've scrimshandered together yourself out of washed-up bones. At the time, though, I didn't think any of this. She was just sort of odd, albeit semi-compelling, and also I knew I'd probably been around people who were odder and had worse intentions, so she was cool, ish, in the scheme of things.

I cut off a triangle of cheesecake with my fork. It was halogen yellow, real airport fare, but even the mediocrity felt so normal that I sort of wanted to cry.

I dabbed up biscuit crumbs with a wetted finger.

'Yeah,' I said. 'OK.'

'You have a house?'

'Kind of.'

'What's *kind of*?'

'Four months behind on rent.'

It wasn't that I didn't have the money: it was just going up my nose or into my liver or into my veins or into my lungs. The bills piled up on my floor, big drifts of dead moths, because they couldn't legally cut off your water, and the electricity and Internet companies gave you a month's grace before remembering to cut you off. If I paid right before the cutoff, it was almost the same as saving money, and the amount saved was worth a bottle of Centenario Reposado a month. The rent pissed me off, even if it was way less than in other places. When my landlord said nothing after two weeks, I inched it to a month; when she said nothing after a month, I pushed it to six weeks. After two months, she sent round the building manager: not to kick me out, just to see if everything was OK. He was a nice man with wire-framed glasses and a sweater whose colour and texture recalled the fuzzy, colouredy static you'd get on old TVs. He said to pay what I could when I could. What I could when I could sounded good to me: it made rent a less urgent expenditure than being out of it all the time. I'd think of the skinny ones and threes left after my outlay on boring non-psychic shit such as food and transport; I'd think of these obliterations in terms of baggies per month, and then go back to spending three or four days in a row bouncing from one couch or bed to another, or passing out on the floors of private galleries or in the corners of warehouses. When I floated home afterwards, I'd be full of this huge elation like my whole body was about to rattle apart, as though I was watching a crime film and waiting for the cops to shoot down the bad guy at the end or whatever; except there hadn't been a crackdown, there hadn't been any cops and, if there had been, the bullets had simply gone through the bad guy as if he were a ghost, and he just went drifting, rising, feet climbing the air, body momentarily light as thistledown. I wanted to see how much I could get away with, then see if I could get out of whatever jam that put me into. I didn't think of this as semi-conscious self-harm: I thought of it as stuff that gave me an adrenal shiver all up and down the front of my ribcage, and I'd decided that this sensation was what marked feeling fully alive.

I forked another triangle of the airport-style cheese-cake and the woman sucked her teeth. 'Well, we'll see about this after the meeting, no?' she said. Then she raised a hand and scribbled in the air for the bill.

She paid and we went around the corner, up Insurgentes a little way, then crossed into Napoles. It wasn't a long walk, but it takes ages in my memory, because the calm and relief in me turned everything to slo-mo Super-8 glow. Next to a dimlit pharmacy there hung a sign with a blue square with the words 'Narcóticos Anonímos' written on it. Below was a doorway with a drawn-up metal shutter, light and cigarette smoke spilling out of it. A group of men and women were settling into chairs, collecting coffees, finishing up phone calls. A couple of them waved to me and smiled even though they didn't know me: except I suppose of course they did, didn't they, because they'd been me, too, at once the centre of the world and one in an infinite series of junkies quivering in the door to waves and smiles from people who didn't know them but who of course did know them, didn't they, and so on and so forth all the way back to the very first meeting.

'Welcome to your house,' Noura said, wiggling her fingers in greeting at a couple of people, then taking a chair in the back row, nearest the door.

I sat down beside her. The plastic chairs were the hardshell ones we'd had in my secondary school. The room smelled the same as the staffroom in that school: cigarette smoke, mingled warm body-fugs, deodorant, perfume. I had that scratchy tiredness where everything feels annoying. So did a lot of the others, sitting there looking twitchy, itchy, thumbs going ninety texting, legs jogging, feet tapping. Two men were talking over one another. Anyone who laughed laughed too loudly. There was no dress code: fancy blazers and sharp pant-suits, scruffy leisurewear, biker gear, fishnet corsets and thigh-high boots. Nobody felt exemplary. Nothing about the room, from the infected-looking plaster to the corded carpet, none of it made me want to stay there. I thought of the ride home and wondered if I could maybe just fucking walk instead. But there weren't any drugs in the room and the strongest liquid in the place was sputtering into a percolator whose jug was patinaed all brownish. The guy manning the coffee station was lorry-ing sugar into a greyed mug pocked with black spatters.

A heavyset man settled himself on a plastic chair at the head of the room and rang a bell with a dainty motion.

'Alright, let's call this meeting to order,' he said. 'I'm Alejandro, I'm an addict. Welcome to the Nuevo Ama-necer meeting of Narcotics Anonymous.'

'Hi, Alejandro,' said the room.

'Hi, Alejandro,' I said.

'Is there anyone here attending their first meeting, or this meeting, for the first time?'

Noura looked at me. So did a couple of others. I put my hand in the air. The room clapped.

'Welcome,' Alejandro said. 'You're the most import-ant person here.'

My nose fizzed. The room blurred. The relief was nothing I've ever felt before or since. It was the inverse of the feeling I'd had when my father had almost caught me in my problem, that jet plane take-off sensation. But this feeling was that same plane landing with a bump, this time finding the surety of solid ground. I remember every word of what Alejandro said. In retrospect, it was boilerplate stuff, guidance for the newcomer, a couple of gnarly anecdotes, some scalding jokes: exactly the kind of routine you do for anyone who comes into a meeting for the first time. But those words are the only text I know off by heart, beginning to end. No poem comes close, no paragraph, no novel's opening, no ending to any short story, because his were the only words that rendered hearing anything else unnecessary. I didn't need to hear anything else. They were the only words that took from me the need to speak. They relieved me of it, released me from that rattly fuckedout language cage. In that moment, it struck me that if I went reading the classics afterwards, hunting for wisdom, I'd simply be reading a turgid paraphrase of what I'd heard from Alejandro. And now here it was, the home feeling I'd been seeking for as long as I could remember. On all those walks – in Barcelona, in Buenos Aires, in Brasília, in Dublin, in this city, even on this walk, the very worst one, after the protest – all I'd really been envying was a cosy hutch that belongs to nowhere in particular: the blue flicker of a TV in the booth of a taxi rank; the book propped on the de la Rosa circles of mazapán and the Bocadín chocolate wafers and the Snickers bars at the corrugated puesto outside a private university; the den of smoke and Futból Azteca that the portero of my first apartment would glower out of, well into the night, watching nothing happen; the four bags amounting to slightly above my bodyweight, still stowed under the stairs, as though I might have to run out of here at a moment's notice, the pollen-textured light over the book-shelves in a corner apartment, a window deep with time, specifically, time deep and quiet and unbroken enough to read every book on that shelf, leave them heaped and discarded on the bank of your own absorption in time as deep as a lake. This was the home feeling I'd been after, all along, and it was here, in this classroom-type meeting space, with its smell of cigarettes and its striplit carpet. I may as well have stayed where I'd begun. They didn't come into being, any of the places I'd been, just for me to come along and take a story out of them. No: the best stories I'd ever find, the stories that'd keep me alive, the stories I could never tell anyone, I'd find them here, in that familiar-fug room and every other room just like that.

The relief: drug-rush, squared, cubed, exponential unto infinity – cooled, cleared, a wind nearly, one that rattled every shutter in my head and my mind and what I guess I maybe have to call a soul. This feeling passed, of course, but the windburned glow it left in me afterwards, it's still there, at least present enough as a memory to keep me coming back. That first meeting, it's that first hit or drink or line, the one that knits up all your problems and makes you feel safer than the womb. None of the other meetings feel the same. You keep upping the dose. You keep chasing that initial high. You dive deeper and deeper into the programme. But you never get back that first-meeting sensation, that rich, delicious hit of belonging, of a comprehension so total that it's a soul X-ray taken by a technician whose intention is only to love. One guy I know says he's going to keep going to meetings until he wants to go to them. I'm keeping going till I get that first feeling back, which I know I'll never get back. But the chase is a reason enough.

*

Noura dropped me home. The portero met me at the door as I was looking for my keys. The look on his face was apologetic.

'They called around while you were gone,' he said. 'The owner and her family, I mean. And. Well.' He lifted my two old sports bags and placed them at my feet. Then he reached behind the door and took out two Amazon boxes, the ones with all my books in them.

'They opened the place up,' he said. 'They found some things.'

'Ah,' I said. Sweat prickled all over my body.

Noura lowered her car window and watched, eyes narrowed against the smoke wafting back from her cigarette.

'You know,' the portero said. 'You know what I mean when I say, "They found some things."'

I saw them in my head: the blood spatter I'd kept meaning to mop off my ceiling, the glass-topped table crosshatched with razor marks from all the lines I'd chopped out, the bin of syrettes and bloodied foil and torn-open baggies, the forest of empties.

'Ah, I do yeah,' I said.

'They called round to let you know,' the portero said. 'They didn't want to kick you out, like I said. You're behind, they said.'

Behind me I heard Noura popping the boot of the car. When I turned around, she was jabbing her thumb behind her. I walked over, dropped the bags in. The portero brought the boxes.

'Well, it's been lovely having you,' he said, and he put his hand out to shake mine.

'I wouldn't,' I said, raising my sticky, dirty palms.

So he bumped his elbow against mine, then went back inside, to his den of Futból Azteca and cigarette smoke.

Noura talked to her boyfriend on the speaker phone she'd hooked up to her car radio, told him what was happening. Of the three of us he sounded most relaxed about the situation.

She took me back south again, as far as Narvarte. Her boyfriend, Omar, was a tanned guy with a sharply sculpted beard and a V-shaped upper body, from what must have been a lot of gym-time.

'Are you in the programme, too?' I said, as he took one box under one arm, and the second under his other arm.

'No, no,' he said. 'I'm completely normal.'

'I took advantage of him,' Noura said, as we followed her into the house. She had the strap of the larger of my sports bags over her shoulder. I was carrying the smaller one.

'And continues to,' he said. He was holding the door open for me with his heel.

She took me to a maid's room on the flat roof. Inside was a single bed and a small desk with an office chair. A router extension blinked in the corner. The room was tiny and snug. I wanted to cry.

'And welcome to your house, again,' Noura said, as Omar held a keyring out to me.

'Front door, azotea door, your door,' he said, counting off the keys. 'Bathroom is a pain in the ass.' He pointed. 'That shed in the corner of the roof.'

'That's no problem,' I said. 'And you aren't afraid I'll rob you or something?'

Omar squinted. Noura shrugged, then said, 'Not really, no.'

'You seem very tired,' Omar said. 'It'd be pretty easy to catch you.'

'You're not wrong,' I said, and sat down on the bed. A clean smell bloomed up.

'There's some plasters and things in that little box under the desk,' Omar said.

'We should let you sleep,' Noura said.

Omar gave me a little military salute, then they got out of there.

The first thing I did was charge my phone and switch it on. The first message to ping was an SMS from Helen; she didn't use the apps for this one.

I'm fine, it read. *Tell my parents nothing.*

Then the string of WhatsApps came in from her ma and da. I hadn't even known they had my number. I must have been an emergency contact – the name and number of someone she'd been going to the protest with.

I texted Helen back saying, *Fine, yeah, but that doesn't answer the question: where are you?* Then I called her ma.

The phone buzzed against my ear, rattling the arm of my glasses.

'Jesus,' I said.

'Excuse me?' said Helen's mother.

'Sorry, one sec.'

I checked the screen: Helen again.

If you listened properly, you'll know where I am. Don't come looking for a while. I'll be OK.

'Have you heard from her?'

'Not a thing,' I said. The lie hurt to get out, even though it came out quick and smooth. But, I think, that's my last big one.

I heard her mother suck in a deep, hard breath, then huff it out in a gust of static.

'Because we have,' the mother said. 'She didn't say much. Just that she was fine. And that she wouldn't be back for a while. And not to worry.'

'Right,' I said, not sure if I should add anything. But then I thought of how my parents would feel in the same situation, and added, 'Look, I mean she told me to say nothing, but she did tell me the exact same thing. Like. I mean. She's alive and, you know. At liberty. Or whatever. So.'

Helen's mother sighed. I could picture her touching the links of her necklace as she tried to hear what she wanted to hear in what I was saying.

'So maybe it's just a holiday,' she said. She'd found what she wanted to hear, I guessed.

'Ah, yeah,' I said. 'Definitely.'

'OK,' she said. 'Yes. And how are you?'

I looked around the room. The walls were breeze-blocks painted with warm pink emulsion. Through the window and the glass section above the door I could see yellow dots of light shimmering in the dark, following a curve that rose towards the hills and dormant volcanoes south of the city. Lights swayed; they could have been boats.

'Oh, yeah,' I said. 'You know.'

'That's good,' her mother said. 'That's a relief. OK. Well, look, if you hear anything.' She was a little brisk now, probably already mentally lining up who else she needed to call, then she hung up.

I fell back on the bed in the same shape as I'd fallen down on the traffic island the night before, arms flung out, a puppet whose strings had been cut. My head thumped in fast time with my heart, but it was a good pain, almost, because I was able to take it. I wasn't running off to numb it. I didn't want to do that anymore. There was no need. The thumping fell quiet after a while, and then the rest of the noise in my head and my body did, too, and then I was gone.

*

As with addiction, so with recovery: I needed to begin with the shit. Sometimes I couldn't even get across the roof to the little hut with the jacks and the shower, so I'd take my syrupy shits right into the scissored-off neck of a water bottle, pour it out when I felt well enough. The vomit was an underground ocean rising up with its stone and sand and rot and bones, coming up out of me all salt. All this time on the drugs I'd wanted to be empty, a vehicle for askesis, finding a void, lingering there, but really I'd been avoiding that void all along, and now here the fuck I was. Evenings were bad. I'd zone out, see things dancing at the foot of my bed, faces cratered and bearded and red, bunched up: Caravaggio's late drunks, the ones who hold heads or giggle when saints are dying. I could only eat white things: rice, peeled apples, cereal left soaking in milk for a long time, the potato filling of quesadillas from a street-corner stall that I could just about make it to. Everything tasted of foil, but the colour made me feel clean. Sometimes I'd get this needling urgency to cram the sandwich-maker in Noura's kitchen with forks, just to bring an end to the all-over feeling of craving, every pore hungry, but I couldn't make it downstairs. When the weather stormed, I'd see other stuff: a hunched pianist, steel-wool beard, playing the storm on a piano, deep rubato for the rolling thunder, his scales rising and turning into the rusted fire escape shackled to the side of an old apartment block I'd had to run out of once. When he turned around to leer at me, he wasn't the bearded guy: he was a child, a bad child, small, pale, his teeth lead nubs, one leg gammy and blemished, that of a burn victim, but he wasn't just a child, he was a scream, the scream that had been rattling at the cores of my bones since I was old enough to want to die, and now it was that scream's birthday or something, and so, although it perhaps should be taller, given it was what, nearly twenty-four or so, this small, awful baby that dances was the humiliating actual size of a pain I mistook for something epic, and my skull would ache from how hard I was clenching my molars against the embarrassment of knowing the full scale of my own pettiness. I'd wake from those visions on the floor, trying to cool my fevers, the grouting between the tiles a pumice texture beneath my cheek. I began to think of how I'd best like to die, thinking of Socrates after he's drunk the hemlock, watching swans lower over him, nuzzling his forearms with their necks, twining their supple whiteness around him, while his gaze drifts past the bodies of his friends and jailers towards stars through the plane trees, until his eyes cloud over completely and that picture blurs.

I felt so old. I'd shut my eyes on those images and loop them one after another until I was able to sleep again, waking only when it was well past noon, with shivers and stiffness and tremors, deep quakes way down inside me, underwater, underground, and nothing to take for it. The chord of light striking the pipes of a refinery made me see Dublin, the copper of a distillery through the poplars, under frigid morning light. I'd get up, get sick, get reading – about Humboldt, mostly, how he'd been to Guanajuato, how he'd described the activity and lights around the smelting cauldron high in a crag of brown rock as being like watching the bioluminescence of germs in the knurls of a molar. He'd said something, too, about how white rivers were the ones that were murky with silt you couldn't see far down into, whereas black rivers let you look all the way down to the shifting layers of silt, heavy with vegetable rot, leaving a clear seam where you're seeing all the stars between the stars that you can't see by looking up at the sky, every dot of light faceted, diamond-bright.

Except to make quick gallops to the tortilleria for the sort of food I could reheat quickly, most days I was too panicked to leave the roof. The mix of light and air pollution was tumbling clouds of hot salt: eye-sting, skin-itch, a fine sticky powder of pure tiredness. I'd wait out the day, reading again, at last: at first the Narcotics Anonymous Basic Text in Spanish, then the books that I'd toted over from Ireland and never gotten around to. I'd sit on the edge of the roof, waggling my legs in space, like I was about to swim off into the air.

When it rained I'd lie cruciform on the warm roof in my underpants and feel the phosphor seethe of the rain batter away all sensation of the post-heroin flu. I bought in a whole load of electrolytes and Tylenol, but the headache and the chalkiness around my throat never seemed to go away. I'd chicken-walk nude and weeping around the room, feeling my muscles tighten, bending me around the need until I thought my filaments would ping apart. No longer buried in the old slush of drink and powders, I started to appreciate how noisy Mexico City really was, how trucks zooming by would shudder the walls. I had to buy earplugs. I phoned in for cheap three-course meals from the little comida corrida place around the corner. I couldn't finish more than one course per go, so each meal would last me all day. My stomach might have shrunk, but there always seemed to be more vomit. I cleaned my sores with rubbing alcohol, resisting the urge to swig from the bottle, the sweetish note of it sending me surfing over whole zones of recollection until the memories made my ribs ache. I woke up with shivers, stiffness and shakes, rising up from way deep within me, and with nothing to take to counter them. Every day was an enemy I had to kill. I'd open my eyes and the day would be standing over me, staring down, unblinking, and somehow I'd have to get out from under the harshness of that gaze. Mostly I waited until it was dark, trying not to think of that first golden hit of the day, the one that'd scatter me to photons. I'd startle out of naps, clouds of butterflies with five-hundred-peso notes for wings blooming up out of snowdrifts of coke and following me out of my sleep, and it'd take me a second of panicky sobbing to remember that those billows weren't there, that my relapse hadn't happened.

Later, then, as the sky browned over, my room had a tea-stained gloom to it. At that hour, I thought of Humboldt at work in the archives of Mexico City, amid that cool leather smell of books: *like the hides*, he writes in a letter, *of the carcasses of all that has been thought and lived and written, cut down, emptied, gutted, cured.* He felt depressed, he wrote, at being cooped up with the anatomical plates and drawings of plants that he had come to study. And so, he writes letters to his friends to put off his work. He writes to Aimé Bonpland, his travelling companion on his Latin American explorations, that he feels in the library much the way they did on the Sargasso Sea, watching a vast elliptical mess of weed, a huge cyst wobbling the surface of the water, caught on the mooring ropes of an abandoned ship that was drifting past them, half-eaten by sea holly. *The flatness of the sea stretched for so many miles*, he writes, *that you would see a flash of lightning but hear no thunder, because the storm was simply too far away.* He writes about his eye tracking always to the window of the city archives, drawn by the rucketing of carts, the yawp of vendors, the shriek of steam-whistles, the wild tolling of bells. He is thinking about the smoky dust of the Templo Mayor blooming up into the evening light after lying there for centuries, and he can hear again the creak of beams and winches levering up chunks of ruin so immense that he feels nature and history blurring into the one impossible catastrophe.

I felt the need for a new language to do justice to what I saw, he writes. *There needs to be a whole phonetics of ruination: fricatives harsh enough to sliver the tongue bloodily in two, plosives and glottals as soft as a cough of ash, or else gurgling for long enough in the mouth to become a noise of floods.* He writes about running his finger along the plates, feeling the raised ink in the whorls of his fingertips, only to look up and see a cap-tured monkey hopping around on her leash at the end of the desk, her own wrinkled finger copying his, taking in a drawing of a picture of the same kind of Brazilian tree as she had been kidnapped from. This came after days bumping north to Guanajuato, knees folded almost all the way to his ribs. *I was a shut book*, he grumbles in another letter.

The first thing he did after resting was to climb the paths all the way up to the brown crags surrounding the city. Zacatón grasses swayed with a seacrash sound. Betelgeuse glimmered on one side, Guanajuato on the other. A sound of cowbells reached him from a cou-ple of fields over, sounding just like the ones he'd hear walking to the university at Jena. In the sputtering torchlight, miners turned great oars through barrels of smoking mercury paste. Silver dots pocked their bodies. Their arms had scales. One man's neck was buckshot all over with pink scarring. Humboldt's stomach flipped fully over. A memory assailed him: striping his own chest with incisions, applying nightcrawlers to the cuts, then electrodes and acids, the pain lifting him for a time above the frowning eaves of the town's apothecaries, above the gloomy arcades and their smell of charcoal smoke. He touches his own forearms where the points of burning silver have tacked to the skins of the men working outside the mines.

While I was living in Jena, he writes, *a thunderstorm struck and killed a farmer and his wife. I went out to look. The man's bones looked shot full of holes. The town was doing the same thing to my soul. I feel it again now, here in the dimness of this library. I have seen waters thick with phosphorescent plant-particles, a foam of light, igniting the mosquitoes clustering in the air. All matter is a pulsating cloud of molecules that consumes and regenerates itself moment by moment, in bright invisible reconfigurations as infinite in their scale and density as the galaxies that bloom, burn, and fade unheard all around – a fluttering conflagration, like the feathery thup of a paraffin lamp.*

My own stillness was in part enforced. During my first three years in Mexico, I lived on no more than six thousand quid a year; in my fourth that went up to eight; since getting off drugs it's never gone any higher than twelve. My rent wasn't low at the time I'm writing about now, so I made that money last by staying as monkish as possible. I suppose the meditation helped, in that I learned to wait out a day without burning through my cash or letting my anger and fear make impulsive decisions for me. I'd pirate books, pirate films, pirate football streams, pirate records, watch the sun come up, watch the sun go down again, chalk each successive non-using day off as a success, no matter how hard the time and the hours abraded on me. It was my only job. It wouldn't matter if the bottom half of me was on fire or if I hadn't gotten a pitch accepted or even seen any-body for a week or whatever: the point was to wake up without being high or drunk and then to go to bed that way, too. That was all that mattered. I started to see that as being the only value of a day, started to see each day clean as a sun-coloured coin dropped into a leather pouch, against the bad days behind and ahead – some-thing to be proud of, something that kept me something like safe.

*

Was it domestic bliss with Noura and her boyfriend? Of course not.

'I love this,' said Noura, flipping through the news on her laptop, reading an alert out loud to me: traffic restrictions in place for the next months to make the air less shit. They're due to expire when the rains come. 'Here we are, twenty-first century, and we depend on the fucking rain god to sort us out like it's the year 1300 or some bullshit.'

All three of us were irritable after a week of wearing beach clothes indoors. Noura's boyfriend Omar mocked my tie-dye vests. I mocked how his shorts made his legs look. A snail epidemic broke out in one of Noura's fishtanks because of a heat-induced algal bloom. I was concerned that flushing them down the toilet would result in mutant snails, having fed on toxic sewage, slithering up our pipes for revenge.

'Then don't rinse food down the sink, maybe,' said Noura, as she smacked the snail net against the rim of the toilet bowl.

Through the window: steel on the skyline. A sky made of glass. The buildings had that external hard-drive shine – deep black, light-drinking. I pictured them shattered and strewn across a chemical-pink desert, imagined that last sunset as a swollen blood yolk. I craved rain to wash away the last residues, a big storm, the kind that cancels all space to a white rumble. I wished I had a girlfriend who I could call, invite over, wished we could stand here and look out on the rain's phosphor seethe, dreaming Noura's sitting room into a cave above a crashing ocean, that serenity feeling becoming our home. But you're not meant to have a serious relationship in your first year clean, so I didn't call anyone. Instead, in those days, I'd drift between reading and sleep, the heat and my headaches enough to have me nodding out as though I'd never gotten off the spike. Heat-dreams rewrote the words I'd read until I could no longer tell where sentence tapered into dream and dream picked up the rest of the story, took it to zanier and more heightened places than the gobshite contemporaries I was reading possibly could. It was good I was pirating them, because they were shite. Best of all was when I'd dream of the pages themselves: burned-out forests under a lagging of snow and ash, sea-roar audible in the middle distance, woven out of the traffic noise and flight paths around and above my apartment.

The air that year was shite, too – white with smog from January onwards. Outside too long without a drink and I'd get an itch in my glottis. Airborne dirt lent my glasses a sepia filter, so I put brown ones on all the time so I didn't see the dirt. The sewage pipes were bursting, too, spills drying, a dirty vapour rising into the air. *Inferno*, the Third Circle: a fine shite drizzle for ever and ever amen.

The heat and the tight oxygen supply made sleep-drop harder and faster and more unpredictable than it ever had even on drugs, thick and powdery and merciful. Since the eighties, the city government had measured air pollution in IMECAs – Índice Metro-politano de la Calidad del Aire ('Metropolitan Index of Air Quality') – according to levels of carbon mon-oxide, ozone and other key pollutants. To my newly unstoned ear that acronym could have been the name of a made-up Indigenous people, named after their tiny white poison arrows, an invented fame that's preserved in the all-angled, flurrying particle blizzard we walk into when we leave our houses.

A measure of fifty IMECAs on the government site meant the air was safe to breathe. Those months the index was at a hundred and fifty. People were talking about it hitting five hundred. I'd squint through my amber-brown lenses at skies that were cotton wad-ded into a bell jar. Maybe one night I'd get that petrol-scented yellow smogweight at the front of my skull, the one that presages migraine, drink the last coolish drink in the house, drowse off watching a download bar, wake up the same as one of those Pompeii cunts, annihilated by the air itself. I'd sip water and chew nicotine gum and try to decide if the evening sky looked closer to an octopus or a manta ray. The livid wedge, the low, hungering loom of the blood-coloured shape: yeah, definitely a manta ray. But it could also be an octopus beak; the lit smoke-plumes from the refinery its tentacles.

The sky was a platinum shimmer: metal particles in combustion, a broken sheet of dazzle. Silver leaves came spinning down from the eucalyptus trees: the worst plant you can have in a city in a dry country – so greedy for water, it would suck up whatever droplets were left in the swamp the Spanish drained after conquering the Aztecs. Their python roots ruck up pavements, burst pipes, bleed us of water. All major cities have a body of water within them, but all of this city's rivers diverted underground to make way for the major eje highways – the arterials. The same word people use for people on life support, they use for those rivers: intubado. The city was sucking its last breaths but over a period of decades rather than hours, so you didn't notice. All geography is a photograph, same as those Hawaiian island chains drifting away from each other, clots of lava floating, darkening, growing trees, the way this place absolutely never will. The city's vast thirst has sucked down most of these aquifers, and now it's starting on the volcanic springs of poor towns in the southwest. The battle for water had already started in villages like San Bartolo Ameyaco, with residents fighting off the police sent to secure water supplies for the city government. Breathing in through my nose gave me an ammoniac tang. I thought of the city's gut-shape on the map, our soured air the ketoacidosis of a gut stuffed on 24 million commuters, their aircon, petrol, cigarettes, labour, their 15kg-per-person of solid waste per day, their 6 million cars, 10 per cent of which are so old – the average age of vehicles in Mexico is seventeen – that they shouldn't be on the road, turning every street into a dry, choking throat.

The horizon was a great white scar. A flare glided over: widening jet contrails the colour of blood.

Vigny and Baudelaire, de L'Isle-Adam and early Mallarmé, they did gnostic riffs on Dante's circles of *Inferno* to talk about the modern city, the shut-in industrial sky appearing to them as the ceiling of a Manichean universe, Satan refigured as a laboratory demiurge experimenting on humanity: '*the low, heavy sky weighs: a cauldron lid,*' says Baudelaire, the best one. But for those *poètes maudits* – 'damned poets': their emo name, not mine – the smog age's first blood suns were the Book of Revelation's red sun, that time in history when an adoration of progress turns to a hubris so vertiginous that we mistake our own burning for a glory dazzle: *And they did cry when they saw the smoke of her burning, saying, 'What city is like unto this great city!'*

*

It perhaps sounds as if I'm complaining, but those roof-top days have a still luminosity to them that makes them exist apart from all of the time either side of them. Time had become a saffron dust that piled up minute by minute at my feet, the same colour as the hazy sunlight in that neighbourhood – with its quietness and palms and cafés on the park that I couldn't afford, the serene lives behind the windows of the apartments that I also couldn't afford suggesting a Sunday-paced life that was nonetheless mine, as though I'd skipped a step, arrived at retirement, could kick back and watch now, read about lives I didn't need to live, didn't even want to live, places I didn't want to see, didn't need to see; they were all in the books. My own life became these other lives hovering around me in the moted light and the words on the page before me, same as when I was a kid, circling back around to that old feeling of everything that happened to me seeming to happen to someone else: as though I'd died already, except in a good way this time.

When the volcano grumbled I'd watch the vermicular spackle of ash caught on the sill writing and rewriting itself. The towers in the pollution-whitened air shimmered. Sometimes all you could see of them were the windows set in the sky, the way the concrete blurred into the tone of the air. Behind my house, the alley fumed: cooking smoke, onions and diced green serrano peppers, the petrol engine that the sculptor behind us used to bend metal fibres unto his will. In a glass box standing at the corner of the azotea was a Santa Muerte statue, black eyes and clamped-shut teeth looking the way I felt, pure being grinding on nothing, a smile that wasn't a smile, just the face you make when the skin's sucked from your bones, an emblem of what it took out of you to live here, air that was acid-stingy nibbling you away, the need and the frenzy and the poverty all around a warning, the city the same shape as a stomach on the map, peristalsis of traffic hitching along its each and every avenue. I'd leave offerings for her, this Lady of Holy Death, the odd time: stiff dead flowers poking rustily up out of a Coke bottle, a jar of rice and grains in packed-tight strata, water and limonada in big tar- ros that seemed filled with cloudy light. Her robes were different colours depending on what her believers were after: red for love problems, green for legal help, blue for protection, black for revenge. Amber is for healing and transformation: recovery colours, deep honey-coloured cape trimmed with purple. According to the lore, the saint wasn't even really a saint: simply a soul in Purga- tory trying to work off a debt by serving others.

Noura would come up to do step work with me, and bring me to meetings if I didn't look too ill. She'd read out the questions in the step working guide, I'd read back the answers. A lot of the time my writing was too squiggly to read. But I had so little in my head that I was able to remember more or less what I'd written. I'd copy down the questions in red, answers in blue, double-space the lines, same as in secondary school. As the letters steadied and began to prop each other up, I started to feel less as if that idea of a body of work wasn't a corpse or corpus but something that could be alive. What that meant, I didn't exactly know, but it felt nice to think so. What felt nicer was that this was the first time I'd written anything in a long time.

At the meetings, before the sharing, there was always this short set of boilerplate readings, the last one titled 'We Do Recover'. It wasn't optimistic. It said, 'We suffer from an illness for which there is no known cure.' I felt that to be true. I had the belief then that being alive was a kind of disease, but a disease with bones. The text continued, 'It can, however, be arrested at some point, and recovery is then possible.' I thought of *Nazis at the Centre of the Earth*, one of those films I'd doze in front of during those nights after the soup run back in college. I remembered the ranks of stormtroopers thawing out at the bottom of a huge shaft under Antarctica, this shiny frozen mass with faces slowly looming out as the meltwater bled through the ice in long gouges, thinning it until they were free, them and their gas masks and machine guns at the ready, the people they shot groaning as bullets ripped through them, their faces looking spasmodically ecstatic, the orchestra giving it all those Bernard Hermann stab-and-jabs. The pain in me felt continuous with that violence, but not as a victim of it, more as the inert stuff that went into making their bullets or weaponry, bad in its raw state, but always available to be made into something worse. That got me down, made me shift on the pebbled seat of that recovery-room chair as member after member took the floor, talking about late recovery problems that felt as vivid and distant and jumpy as the highlights reels of Instagram: 'My husband's annoying me.' 'My boss has me down.' 'Someone backed into my car and I couldn't shake the desire to haul that fucker out of his car, rip his shirt, smash his glasses for him.' 'I'm stressed by my new promotion and it's making me want to take the edge off.'

I'd hold back the shrugs, shift back and forth on the plastic seat, arms folded, thinking to myself, yeah, well, at least you have a husband, or a boss, or a car, or a promotion, or a will to live.

There's a story in Richard Ellmann's biography of James Joyce where he talks about him wearing out the seat of a pair of trousers during his brief stint working as a bank teller in Trieste. This no longer seemed disconcerting or weird to me. I couldn't bear that room, couldn't sit still, but I couldn't leave, either, because I knew the places I'd be beelining towards if I stormed out of there. So, I tried to hold that word 'recovery' in my head, turning it over and over the way people walking through a desert turn a flat pebble over and over, because the cool weight of it feels almost like water. The word followed me home. I'd steal PDFs of etymological dictionaries to see if they might tell me anything. The philologist Skeat called it 'a difficult word'. I couldn't argue. Then he gave it a stab, drew up the word for 'to get well again' in Latin. I hated that. 'Again' didn't apply; I hadn't ever been all that well. How was I going to recognise wellness at all, then? Another dictionary suggested the first use of 'recovery' as a noun in Shakespeare's *All's Well That Ends Well*, where you have a king coming round from an illness, and a guy getting a lost drum back. This gave me nothing. I shut my laptop. There was no way I'd get the lost time back or make up the ground I'd lost on my peers while I was getting fucked up and feeling sorry for myself. I took out the blue book with the basic text, opened up my PDF of the step working guide, copied out more questions, wrote down more answers. All the pain too liquid to be sicked up was sloshing around in me; but writing it down at least tired me out enough to make me want to call that early sobriety desolation by the name *peace*.

One of the days I read out a long answer to one of Noura's questions: something out of Step Three. After I finished she was quiet, waiting for me to continue.

'It's all I've got,' I said, and looked up from my notebook to see her looking at me steadily, sitting forward on one of the plastic faux-Eames chairs she kept on the roof, elbow on her knee, her cigarette burning unsmoked towards the writing.

'What?' I said.

'That was very insightful,' she said. 'And, well, quite gripping.'

'Are you being sarcastic?'

'Not at all. You really got a hold on this one.' She flipped back through the pages of the step working guide. 'Yeah, I mean. Yeah. You've basically nailed all of them.'

'Huh.' I started to go back through the pages, rubbing my fingers over the nubbled surface where I'd been driving the pen into the paper. I hadn't even been worried about what I was saying, or how. I just wanted it out of me. The pages were written to crisped onion-skin – teeming with script, fifty, sixty words a line. There was no style to it, no curlicues, no six-dollar words. Maybe that's why they'd had an impact on her: because I hadn't been trying, because I hadn't been waving my hand in the air looking for an audience, the way I had been before. The only thing I'd been gunning for the whole way along was the empty tired feeling that came when I'd filled a few pages for the day.

'It doesn't feel too special, written down,' I said. 'Just seems sort of small. And not even that bad. But, you know, just also sort of not a big deal or whatever.'

She tapped the ash, took a quick drag that she blew out of the side of her mouth. 'You could probably go straight into Step Four, if you wanted,' she said. 'And you should go away from town for it. A little holiday.'

'And you don't think I'd go AWOL?'

This was day thirty-six. I'd read or heard something about how the first forty days trying to kick something helped to reset your body's relationship to that something. I'd promised myself I could use on day forty-one, but now I couldn't be arsed. Noura wouldn't call me insightful again if I cracked. That word from her was something to lose.

'You might,' she said, 'but you have to test yourself sometimes, no? Hit the beach,' she added, and I could see the one I'd choose: an empty one, way off the drag, somewhere in Veracruz. I'd gone there as part of a job I'd gotten once, working as a risk analyst for renewable-energy companies. They'd wanted to know if places were too dangerous to invest in. They'd send me down, I'd send back a report, they'd decide whether to invest or not. The reports were easy. I'd go to the place, find that it was dangerous, say, 'Yes, it's dangerous', and they'd pay me. But this beach was in a sort of bubble of safety right between two horribly dangerous places.

The bus would get me there in four hours, along the new highway to Tuxpan on the Gulf of Mexico.

'Yeah, OK,' I said. 'OK.'

'Cool,' she said, and clapped her hands on her thighs, standing up from the chair. 'Go check those bus prices.'

*

I had a work trip anyway: I'd make a trip to the coast after I finished filling out the story I was working on. The assignment covered abuse of Central American migrants by Mexican immigration agents. And so, before I headed up the coast to Tuxpan, I visited a migrant shelter in Ixtepec, near the Isthmus of Tehuantepec in Oaxaca. After spending the day listening to dozens of people, I went to bed in the shelter, under cracked windows which had been repaired by pasting obsolete legal testimonies over the gaps. All around me in the dorm, people who I'd interviewed were falling asleep, wiped out by their journeys, the blisters on their heels burst and pulpy, like boiled tomatoes, their soles cured to leather, the setting sun printing shadow-writing from taped-up depositions onto their skin.

The page above my head told the story of six Honduran men hiding from La Migra in a cornfield, who, having thought they were safe, smelled smoke and looked up to see migration agents setting fire to the field.

The narrator of the story – the only one to escape the deportation vans – sustained second-degree burns. I hadn't seen a single report of that case in any newspaper, in any courthouse file. I wasn't going to either: a volunteer at the shelter had told me they wrote up the story of any migrant who wanted to talk, but that it was impossible to secure legal follow-through. Most were too afraid to give names to law enforcement. The rest were too keen to keep moving north.

It was easy to see why: one guy, Leonardo, told me in unbroken Texan-accented English how he'd built a life over the course of fourteen years in the States and had it all come crashing down around him when he'd been pulled over for speeding. Now he was walking all the way through Mexico to avoid the buses, because La Migra was checking them. He couldn't stop showing me pictures of his thirteen-year-old son – still in the US – on his phone: his bobble of curls, his lower teeth bared in a grin as he lifted a dripping spoonful of ice-cream to his mouth.

The story was much the same with Patricia, a bee-keeper from El Salvador whose microfinance loan had vanished into extortion payments to the local gang members whom she'd fled once the money ran out. Her phone was cracked, but you could still make out the sturdy frame and smiling face of the teenage son she'd run away with. On the last night she'd seen him, they'd slept in the upper branches of trees, tied in place by their belts. La Migra had picked him up soon after and promptly deported him. She had no idea where he was – none of their relatives had seen him at the airport in San Salvador.

Earlier in the day the volunteer staff had given me a dental mask to wear while I spoke to people through the bedsheet wall of their makeshift quarantine ward.

From outside came the slap of suds and water hitting concrete as people washed clothes at a common pump. The clotheslines were bright with kids' onesies, with spaghetti-strapped tops, with neon-hued football jerseys for teams from dozens of cities across Central America.

Later that evening I'd stand at the same spot and listen to the noise of crickets and chattering babies all around. A karaoke competition would be thumping away, two Salvadoran drag queens done up in spangles and lip-syncing to the Gloria Trevi song playing on the YouTube window of someone's laptop. While they drew delighted hoots and applause from the crowd, a real-life couple who'd met on the train would be rehearsing verses of a bachata a little way off from the crowd, gearing up to see if they could outdo the drag queens once it was their turn with the karaoke mic.

Watching them, my mind blank, I thought to myself how a year before I'd been working on the same story, sitting under the palapa of a seafood taco place in Saltillo, Coahuila, thousands of miles from Ixtepec, eating a miserable plate of rice and beans drowned in salsa and drinking four, five, six beers. I was thousands of miles from the coast, and yet looking out at the vast desert floor of a long-gone sea, the canyons and stone mountains blurring into the reefs of which they were the remains, the sound of wind a gullsong in the wires, heat-shimmer spreading waterlights above the towering highway overpasses. Just as Dublin is a suburb of a nameless, laminate America, everything in Saltillo felt as though it had been made in the United States, too: the Walmart signs, the Chevys on the road, the migrants making their way to and from the train tracks of La Bestia, the gang members chasing them, all of it a legacy either of the 1980s mass deportations of alleged gang members to their home countries, the 1980s State Department sponsorship of right-wing paramilitaries, or the 1980s outflow of US brand names to everywhere else. Even the story I was writing – about Mexico's Programa Frontera Sur, a 2014 initiative intended to firm up the southern border – even that was made in the US, with funds diverted from the Mérida Initiative, a security cooperation agreement to 'safeguard the human rights of migrants in transit', which was another way of saying that migration agents were raking through buses, pulling people down from trains, chasing them through cornfields in order to deport them before they could join the thousands of people at the US border waiting for their asylum claims to be processed, their throats growing sore from the gelid, bacteria-loaded air conditioning, at the mercy of the guards' moods, their bathroom visits counted, no room to sleep on the floors, their kids dizzy with hunger because the sandwiches they're given twice a day in lieu of meals are frozen in the middle and the wad of cold bread hurts their stomachs. Federal police pickups were all over this city, all over any city that migrants passed through, their blue lights rippling the dark under highways, men and women and children sitting in the back of the jeep with their heads slumped at the feet of the cop manning the tripod and its mounted AR-15-style rifle, passing a large bottle of water back and forth between them. That's how they'd lure you in sometimes, with promises of food and water and medical attention, right when your legs had gone bockety with tiredness, right when your mouth was parched and your throat tight, right when the winding snake of the road truly looked to be without end, right when the notion of going into detention and returning on the plane back to a home that wanted you dead could nearly be thought of as a momentary break, a reset on the game, a chance to regroup and begin walking again.

At the traffic lights up the road from the restaurant where I was sitting, an Afro-Honduran kid of about seventeen, the dense bolus of a rucksack strapped to his back, dressed head to toe in black, went smiling and nodding from car to car, looking to get his battered Krispy Kreme coffee cup filled with change, the wind and the draughts of passing cars drawing whorls and spirals of sand on his clothes. I knew him – I'd talked to him earlier in the day, at the shelter near the train tracks – and now I waved to him from my palapa. He had shown me a Ziploc pouch that he'd pulled out of the inside of his hoodie. Inside was his passport, a photocopy of that passport, his birth certificate, a photocopy of that birth certificate, his school reports going back to when he was twelve, with straight As in everything except for maths, plus a typewritten testimony from a local lawyer who'd done him the favour of attesting that his town was as dangerous as anywhere else in Honduras, that he'd been threatened with racist violence, with being either recruited into a gang or shot in the head, and that his employment prospects – even if he finished school – were to either join a standing army of surplus casual labour, join a gang, or join the broken trails of people making their way out of Guatemala City, Tegu-cigalpa, San Pedro Sula, San Salvador. Purple, yellow and ash-grey residues mingled at the bottom of the envelope. The documents looked decades old, sallowed by the drag of his hands over them.

'I get so afraid I've lost one of them,' he'd said. 'I take them out, I lay them out page by page, I count the pages, then I read them all again, because it's so easy to forget you're someone more than just the road when you're out here.'

I wish I could remember his name. There have been too many names, and for my stories, I had to change all of them. Right then, I was ready to put another dinner on my expenses, anything he wanted, and I felt a lift of goodwill under my ribs thinking how nice a guy I was, but he just beamed back, gave me a big wave and went back to working the cars glinting under the last of the day's sun as they waited for the lights to change.

I looked back around the yard where the women were singing karaoke, under a night that was starting to fall as black and wet as the Lycra pants dripping from the clotheslines, saw kids boogying on the spot, saw mothers shimmying with them, holding their little ones' hands above their heads, saw lone men with pained looks on their faces, thinking of people who weren't there.

I wish I could tell you that in that moment I laid my suffering alongside theirs. I wish I could tell you that I felt shame at the disparity between the two. I wish I could tell you that this disparity snapped me into a new dawn of moral clarity. I wish I could tell you that in this new dawn I felt a fresh impulse to get their truths down as clearly as I could, and thereby make up for the suffering I'd caused by buying drugs from the kind of people who harassed them. Nothing of the sort occurred. I had a job: to listen and to copy down what I heard and to put what I heard in context. I'd been doing that for a long time. It had never once seemed like enough.

In Honduras, in the summer of 2014, I'd met a Garifuna guy called Walter, who told me about the sort of tiny stresses no account of La Bestia can give you any real idea of unless they've been written by a rider on the Train of Death itself. He talked about the stress of chasing after the train when you get down to pee and then need to run to catch up, about how hard it is to find a safe place on the roof, because there's dozens of people scrambling for them, about how you will sit there waiting until the absolute very last moment possible to get down to pee, because the second you do that, your safe spot will be gone. He talked about the schoolyard vibe of banter, bullying, ambient gruffness, everyone with their eyes to the front, their jaws set, clicking their tongues at other people's bathroom habits and noisy food-wrappers and the too-loud music they play on their phones, trying to elevate themselves above their situation by making themselves feel bigger or better than others, everyone crabby with heat, cagey, scared.

I looked back around at the crowd. The weight of everything I'd heard wadded up in a ball inside me and the floor of my stomach felt like it was about to fall out of itself. There was no way to unpick it all and put it into words other people would get. I didn't get it. I'd listened, but I didn't get it. All I'd learned was that

I didn't even get that I didn't get it. Everyone I'd spoken to was a repeat deportee. They'd flung themselves again and again against fences, against border guards, against judges, against courtrooms, and the state let that happen, encouraged it even, allowed them to keep trying to put one foot in front of the other, persisting past all hope, because to be exhausted, to be in despair, to be baffled and confused and lost is precisely the condition that the state wants you to be in, because the fatigue of inertia permits silence, but it's a particular form of silence – that silence of dust and fog blowing over a space that people have been removed from, turning in spirals above the gaps between speech, between words, between paragraphs, silt of a zone in which mourning and grief, horror and despair move breaking over and over one another – fog-shapes, ghosts, then finally nothing. How to do justice to all of what I'd heard in language, and then to polish that language to a tone of reportorial calm, to polish that language into a voice whose underlying vision was one in which crisis was nothing more than a temporary disruption of stability? How to adopt that voice, to feign it, to feel it along my blood, and not feel, too, the teem of everything left out in order to maintain that tone? If I looked back over everything, I couldn't find a time when language cooled or calmed any of that great seethe of details. What language was there, unless it was written in letters that wobbled on their stems, screamed so hard that the hoops of their vowels split open, lay down flat in sobbing illegible heaps, split along the fabric of themselves, and wagged in your face the jut of bone, bloodied, jellied, wet all over?

A memory of running came back to me. I was chasing after a train somewhere outside Apizaco, Tlaxcala, because there were three kids wrapped in blankets – decorated with Princess Jasmine, Moana, the two girls from *Frozen* – who were sitting on the gondola of the train, a man towering above them, head to toe in black, a cagoule over his face against the sand and the wind, the MP5 cradled in his arms that looked so shinily like the ones you see in films that it seemed unreal. I was running because I wanted to see if he had a badge on his uniform, if he was a cop, if he was private security, if he was a trafficker, but then the train pulled through the junction and sped up and I was left with my feet clunking against the heavy stones of the verge, slowing to a halt, my hands on my head, utterly at a loss.

*

After Oaxaca, I went to Veracruz, stayed outside Córdoba, Veracruz, where I met with a group of around twenty-five women who have made food for migrants since 1995. Nicknamed Las Patronas – a pun on the name of their community, 'La Patrona', but also because 'patrona' means 'boss' in Spanish – they make and deliver around three hundred lunches per day. When the train approaches, they take their bags of food and jog down to the bottom of their garden and fling the supplies into the air for migrants to catch as the train slows down past them. In the enormous kitchen, the windows run perpetually with steam from their pots. The meals are hearty, same as you'd get in a three-course comida corrida place in Mexico City: rice, beans and tortillas clapped by hand out of big chunks of masa, along with other guisados – chicken in mole, tortitas de verduras. 'There aren't many people at the moment,' Nila, one of the founding members told me on the day I went to talk to them. 'We're not getting many people on the train. Nobody wants to come through here. There are too many guards further up, where they get on board, and there are new, tall fences with barbed wire around the tracks, too. If you want to get on board yourself, now's a good time: there's plenty of room. You'll get a good seat.'

Out back, two men from Guatemala flung seed for the hens poking around in the cold black dirt. Pigs nuzzled against each other. When I walked over to the place where the women had said the train would be, it was already there, steaming in the light. When I put one foot on the first rung, it felt like ordinary metal. I tried to call up all the voices I'd heard travelling around the country, but none of them would come. It was just me there being on an old computer and clicking on the screen while it was frozen, this dull *tung tung tung* noise in my head as I climbed. I lay down on the roof. The metal was warm, but soaked with rain. As the train began to move, slowly at first, I watched the gravel moving underneath it, a video moving in rewind while the train was another video playing in fast-forward. The only time I felt scared was when I was climbing back down, afraid that I'd roll under the wheels. But even that wasn't so bad. I even enjoyed the drop to the ground, the dull thud the same as when I'd jump off walls as a kid. Already soaked,

I lay there in the wet grass, under the light, watching the train snake past me: the butty head and its wipers swiping through dried-on dirt, the corrugated tanks, the rusted-out dumptruck-looking carriages whose contents I couldn't begin to guess at. Three cars back from the one I'd gotten up on stood a mother in a black coat, the hood lined in faux fur against the foggy cold. She was holding her sleeping kid by the elasticated waistband of his jeans. He hung by the inner curve of his elbows from one rung of the metal ladder, eyes so tired they could have been river pebbles.

*

On my way back, I travelled to Xalapa. The bus went at night past spotlit train yards, bales of razor wire, walls by the railroad tracks so high that none of the migrants would be able to climb them. White, space-cancelling fogs made the road swing in wide curves through colourless nothing. I was thought-free all the way with the Narcotics Anonymous step working guide clutched in my lap, flicking the book's rounded and softened corners. Under the hard last sun fell the day's rain and glazed the main square to an ice rink. Two kids skipped alongside their parents while their dad bobbed a kite just out of reach. From the bandstand came cheap-sounding, violin-led dance music strapped to a thudding, urgent beat, while the shapes of candied fireworks traced the violin sounds through a thrilled hot darkness in my chest. I wanted to write myself empty of every bad memory, gouge divots of self out with the nib of my pen, scrape them off, let them flake down to their nothing all by themselves. The weight of them sloshed in my belly along with the sickly weight I used to get after I'd eaten too many sweets.

The next leg of the drive took me through mountains the shape of broken teeth, green spills of mango trees and cornfields. The mountains back home in Ireland lack drama: worn-down Armorican foldings, landscapes smooth as a seabed, which give you at best a shudder or oscillation in the blood, sideways only, nothing propelling forward, no upward-and-over motion imaginable. These at least had an epic look and feel to them. I continued town by town, unable to find anywhere quiet enough until I got as far as a dirt-coloured beach near a nuclear power plant. There weren't any hotels but I was able to bribe the caretaker at a complex of unfinished holiday villas into letting me stay there and I installed myself with an armful of jalapeño-flavoured crisps in the biggest bags available, a brick of 7/11 coffee and about a dozen cans of Dr Pepper that I couldn't believe I'd found. The electricity came and went, but there was water and sunlight. The shops hadn't much food but what they had wasn't expensive. The NA guide had been written and overwritten so many times that there wasn't any room for my answers: what white spaces I could find were cloudy with erasures. So, I copied the questions out in red and put the answers down in black underneath until the pages of my notebook looked bloody and burned at the same time, like the slicks of mingled ink and blood wiped off skin during tattooing. The caretaker left me alone, apart from to bob his head at me timidly as he passed on his way over to the stand of fruit trees that he was planting in the muck. The water spat out white and cold and stung the cores of my teeth, made me see mountain freshets, green university acres rolling away towards white sun and empty skies.

I felt sure that this was what was waiting for me on the other side of all that writing: a quiet home, living close to the floor, amid tatami mats and low furniture, under dim-wattage lightbulbs and varnish-coloured sunlight through slatted wooden blinds, the cover of a book where nothing happens, in a neighbourhood where nothing happens – no groan of traffic, no yawp of kids, no gaggles of teenagers streeling around, no vendors, no drop-ins, nothing that might make anything happen, just long mornings spent picking from one book to another in a study at the back of a secluded house that opens onto a garden of ferns and banana leaves. You can hear blackbirds. The panic of the night is gone. The day may as well last for ever. From the doorway you can look across a space of porous black flagstones made of volcanic rock and up a series of steps into a raised garden, towards the pale almost-teal of the tall Douglas fir, the fiery yellow stun of a gingko. I'd write for so long without stopping that I'd fall asleep on the sitting-room couch.

One of the nights I'd been watching some Dad-pleasing action film or other and the streaming service had scrolled on to a nature documentary that showed a heron stooping to dabble in blood-coloured water. Clouds of mud bloomed upwards. The heron drew up a chunk of moss. Shaken-free water fell.

I wiped my eyes and kept writing, questions in red, answers in black, the page a mess that made me think of the scuffy aftermath of self-harm, my head a mess too, so wiped out that I felt the pen in my grip slip back and forth between a loaded syringe full of rusty blood and scuzz, the fear flowing in hot channels of magmatic black pulp in and around my heart and lungs, wallowing over the fatty plugs; to keep going I told myself that the pen was a syringe, but of a different kind, one that'd drain the hurt out of me, a nib sunk into the cloacum inside me, a thin high snore sucking up that ink, and then globby letters, a seepage, a dark sparkle. I hallucinated an idea of *poems as test tubes for ash and debris and flinders, coating the clear inner curve of the base – nap as fine as wool. Grit, thought-lint, tiny lightweight brain-shapes webbing light. When agitated you'll hear pebbly nubs shuffle with a lightweight anthracite clink.*

The clinking noise in my head made me imagine the ruin of Xitle, swiped from the map where Mexico City now stood, centuries before Tenochtitlán, destroyed when a volcano blew its top, leaving only the circular stubs of the pyramid at Cuicuilco poking above the yellow and red sea of lava. Centuries later, the dried magma was quarried into the temples and homes of Tenochtitlán, then the Spanish pulled those down and the survivors quarried new homes out of the rubble.

The rain outside was a million typewriters going ballistic. The noise made my chest effervesce. I found myself writing the first consecutive paragraphs I'd penned in years. Where the letters were legible they made me think of the black metal shapes of a collapsed fire escape.

The illegible letters – leaked, runny letters – were broken piping: the sight of them filled my nose with the sulphur smell of old plumbing, everything in them draining out, coughing and gargling their way towards silence. When I was done I dropped the pen and let myself flop back against the couch, just me and the suddenly still air, the crash of the tide, the slow detonation of the sunrise rippling orange towards me over the waters, the striped chimneys of the nuclear plant up on the far end of the spit. And then I went outside, into that sharp, rinsed morning with its clouds the folds of a brain. The wind raked my hair, made a parachute of the Hawaiian shirt I was wearing over my vest. I went down to the beach, sank both of my hands into the wet sand on the shore where I'd washed up and ran my fingers over the weird, morphed stones shucked up here beside me – pebble-sized shatters, odd almost-inscriptions of black dirt and mould caught in the brittle page of a razorshell. If I ever used words to tell something again I would want to linger in that moment, remember it all again and again, on a loop, a million different ways until all of it rippled in my nerves: that molten-glass feeling in my veins, my chest going up and down like I'd just run a marathon, sucking on the raw salt tang of the air as hard as I'd ever sucked on a bottle. Little blue crabs scurried through the marram grass from one hummock to another, their claws in the air. I lay back on the cool sand, my limbs star-shaped, under the huge igniting sky – purple reefs of cloud, rippling flaws of deepest red. There was a wind inside me, a lake in motion, the surface tossed into glitter and foam, my blood quick with it. If that wasn't happiness, it'd have to do till my real happiness came along.

*

After I finished typing up this dross, me and my tatty thumbs, my junkie fingers, I climbed up a hill called Cerro de las Culebras, in Coatepec. The cobbles were lead-coloured underfoot: coals burned down to ash, to heatless nothing, or as close as you can get to that. My feet ached around each cool round. Cool smells: leaf mould, soaked earth, pools of rainwater gargling at my feet. Uphill was a leaf tunnel: orchids, lilac gardenias, bird-of-paradise flowers. The begonias' deckled leaf-edges made me think of the interiors of lungs that have been cleaned out. Life can defeat memory. The green tint of all these stems hisses against my ear. All down the scars of my forearms flowed moisture and damp-ness and raindrips. Wet stone gave up a river odour. Fog dripped from ferns, from banana leaves, from the long fronds of the palms. I could taste the fog in my mouth and throat and feel the wet cottonwool weight of it in my lungs as I climbed. My hamstrings had that rage burn in them. A handful of days more and I'd be longer off the powder than I was ever on it, but the death I still want has a smoke-tang to it, a death that consisted in throwing myself down under a palm tree, light splitting fronds into a crown of nine perfect white prongs, my head's final transmission dying to a burble that not even I'm arsed listening to – never have been, actually, all along.

223

All I have for you is the only story I have in me. This story is all that's happening. This story will be happening in me for ever. This story ends with a full-stop that's a hole that's a black pool in me for ever and ever amen. The black pool is in me and the black pool is with me for ever and ever. Black pool, I go back to you: you await. You remain. I wanted no more of any of it – no more words, not mine, not anyone else's, not one more account of clouds' frail architectures, not one more *Change Your Life!* pep talk by some sub-Rilkean MFA creep who's blacked out maybe twice in his life and now knows everything about drugs, the stupid cunt, not one more image of a plumped-up sail, not one more feeling bagged up by some other rube looking to buy some bullshit with the poetic coin they got back out of the change-machine. Stupid cunts.

Tiny flies hovered by the orchids, bodies an old-photograph blue: all the old pictures in my head, those encyclopaedias, those album sleeves, their empty promises, their hope uplift, all of it peeling and curling and floating away. Silence: my ladder out, one foot, first rung. The track curved uphill through a pattering noise: more fog tipping from the eaves. When I got to the top I found a bench, under a rusted tin roof that was held up by four brick columns, the red of them long gone black in the air's moisture. I couldn't bear any of it anymore. I sat there with the cold metal slats under my arse for as long as I could, until I was nothing more than a numb pinging of atoms around and around under skin I was no longer able to feel. Fog broke in slow waves across the wooded face of the mountain. Rain fell for a while, perforated the hanging clouds, died to a loose clatter, the clatter dying in turn to a tick of drops, finally diminishing to nothing. Gradually, below, the orb-shaped lights of the town seemed to bob free of their lampposts and hover in the fog. Then came the bloodslick of the brake lights, reddening the clean wet black of the buildings.

I pushed myself up from the bench and I put my hat on and I went back down the glossy windings of the track downhill to go find something to eat then go sleep at my hotel. Words floated up. I argued with them. *What drives me mad keeps me together.* Or maybe just keeps me from something worse. *Who is it that drags this corpse around.* Fucked if I know. Fucked if I know anything at all, learned anything at all. All I learned from suffering is that I don't like suffering. *I write to forget.* I have learned nothing. I forgive none of you.

Walking out of the campus the night Barry found me on the roof was like skating on a pair of razor blades, going fast, head down, runaway speed, escape velocity: but only as far as a cowled skull that loomed out of the dark, teeth black as watermelon seeds grinning in that bone mouth, and my spine turned to water and my feet went numb in their boots. But when I pasted myself against the brick wall and caught my breath I saw it was nothing more than the big white 'P' of a parking meter. My forehead was greasy. I thought my body might poof away, a cloud of thistledown. The brickwork was dirty past the colour of brick and into the colour of ink. It was like walking around inside a forgotten book, steps clomping lonely in the corridors of the sentences, in the empty whiteness of the space around the paragraphs. Even the stars had a correcting-fluid blotchiness to them.

I wanted to be with my friends, the ones who'd gone to London or Korea or Harvard or even just back home to the gaff of their ma and da, all of us going at it hard, talking shite, smoky dark churning outside, the LCD fire of the heater blasting, a proper session, worthy of the heft that was in the word itself, *session*, the weight of it against the ear a book or blueprint being planked down on a table: a proper day's work, *session*, the lot of us milling through twenty-four packs of Bud and crushed-up blue pills, continuing deep into the fuggy morning, resorting to whatever drink we could pick up when the offy opened, crap cans, worse cava, a pink foam that matched the fizzing texture of my brain, the smoke of cigarettes and joints fraying up in silver threads, reknitting against the ceiling, an unwatched film playing in the background, ads showing shots of Southeast Asian getaways and all that, cars cruising smoothly through evocative European nowheres – twinkling Italian seas, deep pine forests, sandstone city centres with loggias and cafés with hipster Edison bulbs and maple floors and steaming espresso machines, making us the kind of people who could afford to belong in those places, all of it making me feel safely cradled in the dark sway of something.

I hadn't slept in about four days. At that time, I was drinking with anyone who'd have me, even if they'd barely have me. There'd been one party two nights before, at a basement apartment somewhere in Rathmines or Rathgar, hosted by an aggressive man whose large white teeth and bleached Billy Idol hair made him morph every second blink into a cartoon polar bear. The guests were the kind of people I was afraid of becoming, but was rapidly becoming, these party denizens going at it on a week night, well past the excuse of studenthood. I'd taken one suck too many on too strong a joint, felt myself haunted by the impression that I'd fallen among sharks, was turning end over end through smoky billows of sand towards the sea floor: but laughing, laughing over the fear that was thrumming in my chest, a taut wire humming with current. When I'd gotten home, afraid of the weight of paranoia and unwanted pictures tugging me into sleep, I'd gone to the freezer, taken out the foil-wrapped blotter of acid I'd been gifted by a friend. My hallucination had been a scramble of all my PhD reading: an enormous gold and black metal gate made up of images from Dante, a fractal intaglio that seemed to both scroll downwards and move downwards the more I stared. A mist rolled from the metal, but I felt the mist as music, a huge golden chord on brass, supported by silver cables of tremulous violins that glittered in my head like the mooring cables of the barrage balloons that Marcel Proust was staring up at, wearing one of his scorched cardigans, on a crazy night-time promenade through Paris during the bombardment. From his letters and in the background of the brothel scene in *Le Temps retrouvé* there rises a lunar, silvery nowhere, spotlights criss-crossing the clouds, shells whining, the mesh nets of the barrage balloons glinting, the rim of his hat caught all over with shrapnel. *I can barely see*, he'd told Céleste, his housekeeper, when she'd received him angrily at the door, *so I found it all quite beautiful*. After a while this image became a stone mural showing Socrates and Avicenna, their eyes white, no iris or pupil, their words written behind them in strikes of lightning that struck with each jolt of my heartbeat.

The sirens wailing up and down Pearse Street turned to arias against my ears, creeping me out. To this day, when I'm back in Dublin, I can't go down to the part of the campus where I was living when that happened. The tall, dark brick building, the narrow passage, the diagonal criss-cross of the metal stairs: it's the same as looking up at a crime scene, in the moments before I go in and see the body on the floor, the blood spread out in a glistening map beneath the head, and all the sad debris that made up a life – shaver head, comb, toothbrush, postcards, books, beloved kitsch geegaws from other people's holidays – now loosening out of the hold the dead's attention once had upon them. I can remember the sensation of lying down on the floor, with Mussorgsky's *The Great Gate of Kyev* spreading loud gold chords around me, the violins petering down in silver ribbons, and another gate flowing through my head: Rodin's *The Gates of Hell*, zoomed in all big, the twisting bronze-gold bodies, the flames of erotic darkness behind and beyond. How long this went on for I have no idea. The next memory to come is of myself pissing, robe open, into the toilet, munching a wedge of microwaved Quorn, watching my jaws circle ruminatively in the mirror, bewildered by how my head could be so loud and my face so calm at the same time.

Back from the toilet, the food a wad in my gut, I put on The Beatles and tried to spiral out in the Technicolor blue feelings their album covers gave me – *Sgt. Pepper*, *Abbey Road*. Those skies were as warm and rich as childhood skies. When I was a teenager I'd sit beside my mother at the kitchen table under the buttery sunlight of wherever we were on holiday and I'd write and write, as if the pen would never stop, listening to a Beatles best-of a pal had burned for me on my Discman, feeling as though the four of them were playing in the next room. The Beatles would save me. I'd be safe with them. But the safety feeling didn't come. I seemed to have put my foot through the delicate pane of that memory and left a massive fucking hole in it. I became trapped in a cartoon version of them straphanging with Charles Manson on a scuzzy New York subway. They were giggling at me. They were talking about a smell. 'This chap's really weird,' Paul said to Manson, who nodded wildly in agreement. 'He smells worse than a lad on fire, mate,' John said. 'OK, you guys stop,' I said, and flapped my hand at the vision, and knocked over a bottle of Sancerre, but managed to catch it before it spilled, then rinsed away the bad images with so many belts of that white-wine electricity taste that I had spiralled out into a brief moment before John Lennon had done snickering at me.

Unable to sleep, I made coffee, but the boiling water opened a hairline crack in the French press and a magmatic glaur had spilled everywhere, looking like the filth under the ground gouged up by the roadworks outside my flat. I'd stared at the spill and felt it become very, very deep. I should have stayed at home, watched something on my laptop, but screens were causing me all sorts of problems. A couple of days before I had gone for a coffee with my friend, Anton, who was trying to get an application for a doctorate in Film Studies together. Mostly he was at home, working on the proposal, but he was in town to collect his dole, so we'd gone to a café with a TV. This was a mistake. The TV was showing news footage of Colonel Gaddafi being brutalised and murdered by a crowd of people.

'Jesus,' I said, lowering my cup to the table as the footage looped back around again: the hollering crowd, the bloodied mop of hair and beard, his sobbing and dizzy reeling, the string of reddened phlegm lengthening and breaking from his lips, then the dog-yowl when someone lashes a bayonet up his arse, then everyone laughing.

The cries, the blood pissing out of the crease in his head, the soaked wool of his beard and hair, the laughter that shows teeth: it all kept coming, while Kay Burleigh or whoever uttered stilted, titillated platitudes.

'It's fucked up,' I said.

Anton spread his hands and sighed through his nose.

'We should get these in to-go cups,' I said, pointing to the coffees. 'I can't be watching this.'

Anton gave me the finger-guns, then got up to get the cups. We walked south towards the canal at Rathmines. The water was gluey with whorls of caught trash – johnnies, twigs, cans.

'I think I'm depressed,' I said, rapping my heel against a frozen-over puddle, while Anton paused to light a rollie.

'All depression,' Anton said, his lighter flicking, 'is nothing more than regret at one's failure to self-immolate in front of the Dáil.'

'It's true,' I said, thinking how sometimes I'd drink at a bar across the road from the Occupy Dame Street encampment. Last time I'd been the night was oily, the muck a purple lacquer on the tarmac. How the people in the tents could sleep with all that noise and cold, I had no idea: even with my double glazing and central heating the roadworks had my nerves on the edge of corkscrewing out through my skin. Black sacking and tent walls inhaled and exhaled, the folds shining. The fences they'd put up were beginning to blacken with damp. The national debt wavered on the Central Bank building in a bluish projection, a clock that ticked upwards second after second. Some of the occupiers were in here, too, huddled up in the clamshell glow of their laptops, thawing out over hotpots and plates of halogen-yellow chips, their beanies and hoodies steaming on the chairs behind them. A couple of them were talking about people who'd filtered off to Rojava.

'Same as the International Brigades in Spain,' one woman said.

Someone else clicked his tongue and said, 'They can't even decide if unions are good. Nobody says "comrade". It's motivational slogans everywhere. Pure optimism of the intellect.'

Kurdistan, I thought. I wouldn't be able to hack Rojava. I hadn't even been able to hack the sit-in at Merrion Row. The day the police had smashed the protests had gotten to me. We'd started off fairly jubilant, all that cheesy, stirring chanting and drumming that sounded almost the same as the football, streaming along Nassau Street past stony-faced clerks, under trees that still had the blaze of autumn on them, the odd anarcho-syndicalist flag swaying starkly above the crowd. The worst thing, I joked to myself, was probably going to be the sore throat I'd get from chanting stuff like *REST IN PEACE MY FUTURE* along with everybody else.

I went as far as the sit-in, but then started to see people sucked in through the wall of shields, as though they'd been guzzled by a monster. I'd seen guards pulling two girls in by their ankles, and a third go in by her auburn hair. A horse had knocked one guy over, shoving into him with its chest. Some teenagers on the periphery of the crowd were flinging milk cartons, eggs, plastic bottles, all of that, but that was nothing compared to the horses trotting towards us – not even galloping – and the vans closing in behind them, and the guards in fluorescent vests behind them, one phalanx after another, their riot shields and shiny visors dripping with yolk. It had felt like we were at the start of something, but then they'd mounted up and moved on us. The shock of seeing cops drop the mask and run at us, shouting at us to fuck away out of there with their batons working up and down mechanically had felt juvenile, even while the shock of it was still rippling through me. At first the yells were more surprise and dismay than fear or anger, but then the horses had started clopping towards us and then it was just the clatter of retreating feet and people yelping in genuine terror. I tried to imagine how much scarier it'd be if the cops were really trying. When I'd decided I'd had enough I'd turned around and nearly bumped into a lad staggering around with blood running down his face. My feet slipped on the pulp of red and yellow leaves heaped by the kerb. I noticed that the Viking Splash tourist buses were still rolling. A few on the top deck were up on their feet, filming us. Then the lights changed and they moved on to the next stop with a stagey Viking yawp.

'They hit us hard when we were after so little,' I said, as Anton and I walked along the canal.

'Maybe we need to get used to that.'

233

'Yeah,' I said. 'Will you roll us one, too?'

'Do you want me to smoke it for you also?' Anton said, taking the spare he'd rolled from behind his ear.

'Sorry.'

I can't remember what else we got up to. If Anton's dole lasted the day, we were lucky. I lived for these blowouts, which left me totalled the day after, destroyed into perfect consciousness, watching the clouds spin and re-form in the high empty blue of the air, while the Spire turned orange in the sunset of a day I had barely felt.

So, I pulled myself together enough to go over for my shift at the mental health charity, figuring it'd be a good distraction to be around people, but I had to go home early because one of the employees was showing me stuff about Burning Man and it had made me cry, even though I honestly thought it was shite. On my way home I'd run into a friend who still had some pills left over so we'd done them at his house and now I was charging home on my fourth day awake on the trot. The streets stank, a saltfish odour that stung my sinuses.

By now my steps had powered me beyond a big Virgin Mary and onto a beach, and I was marching across the hide of kelp that coated the sand, past the new flats that resembled the dragmarks of a printer error against the blank page of the clouds. Some hurricane or other had dragged its tail through the city, flinging reddish Sahara grit over everything. A vermicular spackle coated the bonnets of cars. The moon was a bloodshot eye. The salt tang of the air grew stronger as I moved through brick warrens of streets towards the water.

Through the upstairs window of one of the seafront houses I saw an older woman reading under the amber glow of a light that fell on her loaded bookshelves and I felt a glum pebble drop into the pit of my stomach. I'd never get through all my books. The lines on the pages were the streets of a city that I was sifting back and forth and up and down against the walls of, grey ash in an urn, marking time until I finally stilled. I looked up at an ad hoarding with no panels left in it. Tatters of black plastic hung in three Y-shapes from the struts. This felt like a queasy omen to me, but then the elation of the empty-stomach drink hit and I spat a laugh at the sight instead, before continuing up the strand, heading for the cliffs.

I swayed at their summit, feeling their outlines resolve into soundwaves beneath my feet. The wind made swallowtails of my greatcoat and chased the tassels of my scarf ticklishly against my cheek. The black and white nothing feeling of it all made me think of Proust – wet eyed, ashen faced – with Bergson beside a window, swapping earplug tips and cures for insomnia, looking down over the recovering post-war city, with its dinner parties and raucous clubs that still felt somehow as though they ought to be impossible, the two writers haggard and hunched in their long coats, cormorants fixing to swoop.

I had another belt from the Green Spot. I could nearly hear the beach quietly arranging and rearranging itself, wind combing sand, tides lifting pebbles, making them clack. I knew how I looked. I was just a bunch of literary precedents stuck together. I'd become a story, and I felt fairly sure that I knew what kind of story it was, because I'd read versions of myself written into life by Dostoevsky and Barbusse and Gide and Nizan: the superfluous, overeducated young idiot who hadn't been consumed by a war or a revolution, and whose days were matches struck one by one and flicked into the dark. Pick up the end of any century and you'd shake out a million of me.

Another swig went into me, another rehashed, late-nineteenth-century sigh went out. I could see boats, poignant dabs of yellow on the sea's engulfing black. Some cormorants driven insane by the light pollution over by a fenced lot were diving from the rocks. The sea was saying *Go on, go on,* and every dark dragback of the tide made me inch closer to the edge. I watched the ragged cormorants and thought of Ovid, of the poet and magician Aeacus, so stricken by grief that he jumps off a cliff, but is transformed into a cormorant before he can hit the water. A plume of foam rose and his body sleeked into the curve of the seabird's neck. My favourite thing about the myth is that he doesn't transform completely: he keeps on diving, driven on by that wish to die even in his new form. A need bigger than him was using his body for him, and this smashed his story free of the self-satisfied narrative shape of redemption by transition.

It was only cowardice holding me back from the second step off the edge. Sometimes I'd lift my foot into the void. I did it now. Standing on one foot, above the shimmering water, I took another slug of the Green Spot, tottered, tried to fall back, heard a sob break from my mouth, saw a brief frame from *Alvin and the Chipmunks* where one of them tumbles off a pier and into deep blue water, scrabbling for his glasses. He says aloud, *My glasses*, and the words go up in a cloud of bubbles. I caught my footing, flattened myself to the outcrop with all the fossils. I didn't really want to die. I was just setting up the circumstances in which I might die by accident. I imagined the dumb look on my face when people pulled me green and bloated and fish-nibbled out of the sea whatever number of days after I was reported missing. I steadied myself, took another belt of whiskey, hugged the outcrop and felt a gloved hand grip the inner fold of my elbow. I looked up and saw Marcel Proust looking back at me with a frown of mild concern on his face.

'The world is as old as we are.'

'Then why am I so convinced it's about to end all the time?'

'Well, you know.' He splayed his fingers in a fan towards the tattered plastic bag of beer cans that was flapping from my open satchel.

'Yeah, alright.'

'It's the noise, I know,' he said. He took an earplug from his pocket, the wide end rimmed brownish with wax. 'Quies brand. Although any will do.'

'Cheers, man.' I looked out at the sea again and swayed. 'What brings you here, anyway?'

'Can't sleep,' he said. 'A strange woman has chosen to make her home in my brain. And the pain of a treatment from the doctors has left me awake for days, aphasiac with the burning feeling, epiphanies moving and turning in my head, gold and black, but wordless, like the scrolling of some ornate door I can't open. So, I am trying to walk it off.'

'Is that safe?'

He bobbed his head a little, weighing it up. 'You get used to the dizziness. It even becomes enjoyable, almost, after a while. I love the blur between turning my head and the things around me catching up. I had been trying to write it off, but nothing in me went still. Living isn't always so easy. I am so afraid of dying before I finish this book that I steam my post to kill whatever bugs there might be inside.' He rubbed his eyes. 'I wrote to a young man whom I thought had plagiarised me. His reply made it clear that he hadn't read a word I'd written, in fact. Which perhaps gives me certain melancholy proof as to the accuracy of what I've said about death and its aftermath and so on.'

'Well, one day at a time,' I said.

'It's been this way for thirteen years.'

'Huh,' I said. Everything was zooming out and then back in again very quickly. My heartbeat shook my whole neck.

The burned ends of Proust's cardigan sleeve were catching on the wind. His eyes and drooping moustache made me think of a long-haired dachshund. He gripped my arm with his hand and eased me back down the slope. 'Dead though I am,' he said, 'I can still help you back to the tomb.'

'That would be class, brother,' I said, and clambered up to my feet, then let him lead me back down the rocks. I hadn't even gone up that high, I now saw. I'd probably just have gotten wet.

'You don't want to risk it, all the same,' said Proust.

'Yeah. Fair.'

'Do you know,' he said, 'what the last words I wrote were?'

'The bit about the stilts, I assume.'

He shook his head. 'So, what I had believed to be nothing to me had turned out to be, in fact, the whole of my life. How opaque we are to ourselves.'

'Pretty. Bleak.'

Proust nodded. 'You never finish at the end,' he said. 'You get cut off. Sometimes you die before you're dead, then you get to live an aftermath, be a kind of ghost of your own life. Wouldn't that be nice?'

The walk took us past Boland's Mills, crumbling and golden on the water. LIVE DUBLIN DIE YOUNG was scrawled in tall red letters on the walls, their reflection wobbling in the waters off Grand Canal Dock. The new buildings were stacked ice cubes. I saw people moving around in beige, minimal kitchens, drinking smoothies, looking down at us. I stopped and put my hands on my hips and clucked my tongue and said, 'It's fucked, Marcel, that's what it is.'

'What now?'

'Just . . . *this*.' I flapped a hand at the LIVE DUBLIN DIE YOUNG graffiti. 'If I put those words in a novel, people would say it was too on the nose. Our hallowed, failed laboratory of revolution, blasted out, blackened, leaving only charred stubs and a carpet of cinders, let go to shite in a tech quarter that's making it impossible to live here. And with that written on the side of it.'

'You should write that down.'

'You think it's good?'

'Not especially, but it might keep you from saying it.'

Clouds roiled above the city. Counterglow pulsed.

'That must be how we look to God,' Proust said.

'Never heard of him,' I said.

He tutted. Even my hallucinations were bored of me.

'Are you feeling better?' he said, as he touched the ring on his blue-gloved finger.

I hugged myself against the cold, shrugged. There was a shallow gargling of water.

Proust narrowed his eyes at the water. Bands of light like copper wire moved on the artificial lake outside the Bórd Gáis Theatre, where they had the book awards. The red neons had a bleary look to them.

Proust was looking at me fixedly, eyes black and beady as those of the swooping cormorants. 'You lost someone, didn't you?'

'It was just a college relationship, Marcel, honestly; they're supposed to be blown out of proportion.'

'How was she?'

'Rich. English.'

He wrinkled his nose.

'Sorry,' I said.

'It's so hard to run to keep up with people who have money. I remember I used to seem to myself as though every time I left the house I was running up – permit the colloquialisms; this is you doing me, the me in your head, your version of me, you scumbag, you inarticulate, and not me tout court – a hundred-thousand-franc debt.'

'This is because you did, Marcel.'

The sun was coming up, white reflected lattices turning and bobbing. There was heat in it. I turned my face towards the heat.

'You really do have to hand it to that sunrise,' I said, swaying.

'Those colours don't work together,' said Proust.

'And it's a bit over the top,' I said. 'A bit . . . loud.'

'And yet,' said Proust.

'And yet,' I said.

I saw his room, the four pieces of black furniture, the drawn curtains, the green glow of the banker's lamp on his bedside table, with no books by other people, just his own lilac notebook. He was writing the word 'FIN' in tapery letters and holding it up with a grin to Céleste, his housekeeper, as she arrived with the morning café au lait.

I turned to ask Proust if calling Dublin 'Cirrhosis-upon-Sea' was funny or trite, but he wasn't there anymore. I eased myself down on a bench, too wired to feel cold. I put my face to the sky. I was drinking the dark as it leaked out into the peachy light. I was something out of bad Verlaine, or worse Mallarmé, but it was all I had in the tank. The stars flowed down my throat, and then I realised I was drinking a bottle of Huzzar that I did not remember nicking from the security booth. I would need to finish it before the commuters started to turn up, finish it and get out of there. I put my hands to fumble for the wax earplugs that Proust had given me, but they must have fallen out. I tilted the bottle to my lips and drank and felt my body sing with the burn of it.

The waters of the tech quarter sloshed back and forth, back and forth – tideless, tedious. And a cormorant dived splashlessly from the bleary red neons into the black pool beneath.

Acknowledgements

As ever, deepest thanks are due to Federico Andornino and Eleanor Birne, as well as Katie Espiner, Holly Knox and everyone else at the mothership, without whom this would be impossible. Your patience and care are never forgotten. It was a tough process, but you brought me back from the edge a lot of times. Much love.

Brendan Barrington at the *Dublin Review* helped me enormously in the writing of three essays that became the heart of this book. I never thought I would be able to get all this stuff out: my deepest thanks. Aliana Santana helped me find the voice underneath the other melling voices: gracias, gracias.

My mother, father, and sister as well as my extended family are the net under all of this: I'm very lucky and grateful. A big hug to Tom and Shwaita and Kali.

I am grateful to the Arts Council of Ireland for their continued generous support. In 2020, I hit a financial wall, and Eileen Gunn of the RLF helped me with the application process for a J. B. Priestley Award. I want to express my gratitude to her.

Beatrice and Naila, Rasika and Maria, Manju and Emma at the Fundazione Santa Maddalena made sure I didn't lose it towards the very end of this: mille grazie both for your hospitality and for bringing Clothilde into my life. Aníbal, Jan, Alessandro, Pablo, Danae – for your company and friendship. Jack for both these things and also the tunes.

Nora, Patricia, Cheik and all at the Centre Culturel Irlandais did more for me than I can credit, as did Shane O'Driscoll, Fionn Foley, Bantum, Karl Geary, Hugh Farrell, Judith Mok, and Michael O'Loughlin. Everyone at Momo's.

I can't count my friends or measure my luck. I leave many out on this page but not off it, I hope.

Tommy Karshan for his steadying presence. Cathal Wogan for keeping the loneliness at bay while I was in England. Ben Pester for his unwavering, generous presence. Tom Watson for being the king of the lads. Jane Deasy for her music and her kindness. May-Lan Tan and Liam Cagney for exceptional walks.

Sean, Lisa, Novak, Colin, Paul, Oisin, Karl, James and Aimee, Killian, Roisin, JP: for ensuring my continued men's mental health. The culvert abides.

Liam, Catherine, Seán and all at Tolka. Dean Browne. Laura Cassidy. Jess Traynor. Wendy Erskine. Georgie and Leeanne. Adam Foulds. Tiffany Atkinson.

The much-missed Mexico crew. Frank, Jovi, Yoyo, Azalea, Levi, Billy. Luis. Julián, Mica, Darwin. Diego, Lucía. Rodrigo, Natalia. Chris. Brendan. Michael, Ursula, Theo. Kyle. Mariana. Gustavo. Edu. Magda. Janet. Doug.

So, so many thanks to Hugo and Dennis for shelter. Vicki and Daniel. Kosha and Benoît. Pickle and Stuart. Lovely Raph.

The Jardin de Luxembourg Ping-Pong Club. France Jaigu. All the friends of Bill W and Doctor Bob, the friends of Jimmy K: in London, in Dublin, in Paris, in Berlin – even in Norwich. You keep me alive: sorry about that.

And after everyone here but before everyone everywhere else – Quinnie, love: if I didn't have you in my life every day I'd be half-alive. I can't believe my luck in finding you. I'm boundlessly grateful for all that you are, and also for all the laughs that you and Hugo and Eva bring to me. I haven't the words. I'll leave it there.